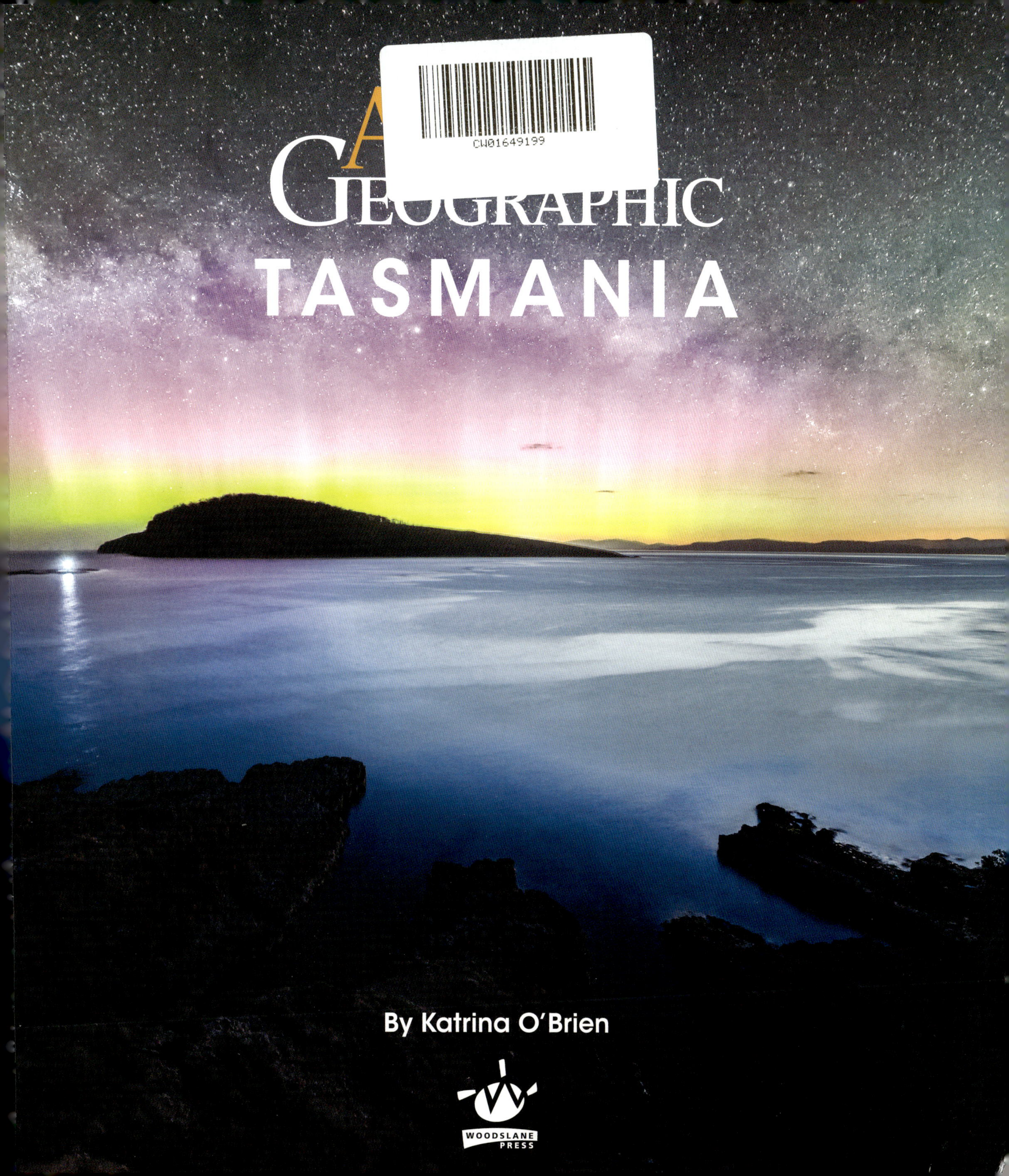

A GEOGRAPHIC
TASMANIA

By Katrina O'Brien

WOODSLANE PRESS

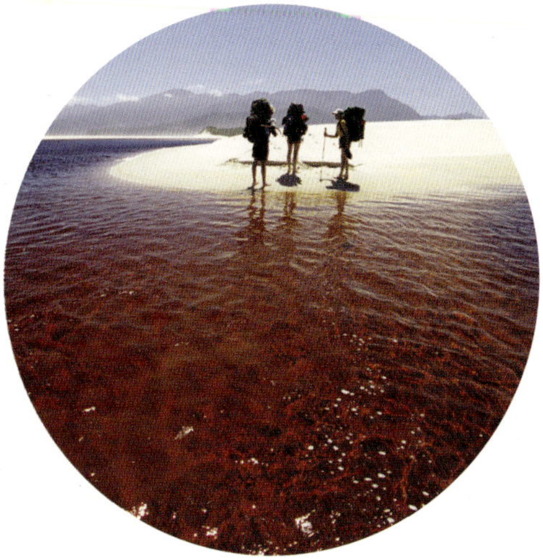

Woodslane Press Pty Ltd
10 Apollo Street
Warriewood, NSW 2102
Email: info@woodslane.com.au
Tel: 02 8445 2300 Website: www.woodslane.com.au

First published in Australia in 2018 by Woodslane Press in association with Australian Geographic

(see acknowledgements on page 62)

NATIONAL LIBRARY OF AUSTRALIA

A catalogue record for this book is available from the National Library of Australia

Printed in China by Asia Pacific Offset
Cover image: Mount Pegasus north in the Western Arthur Range by Luke Tscharke/Australian Geographic
Back cover: Cameron Cope/Australian Geographic (Preservation Island in the Furneaux Group)
Book design by: Christine Schiedel

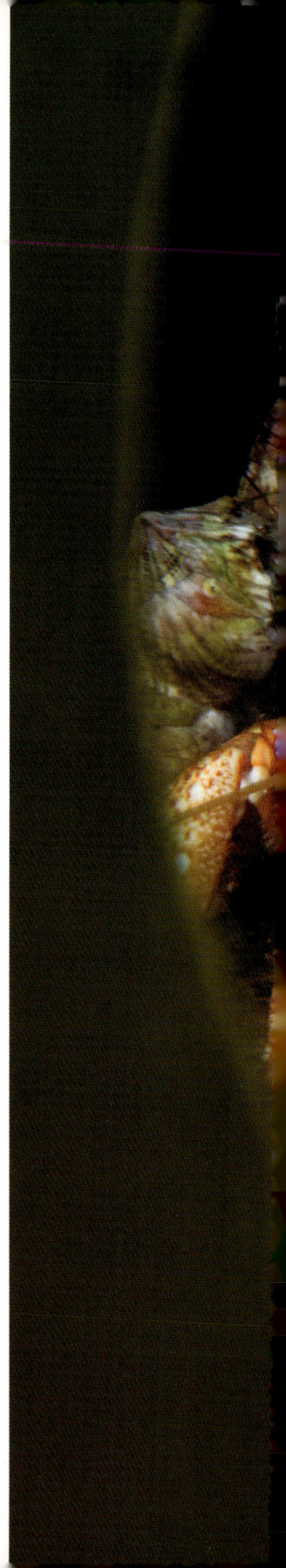

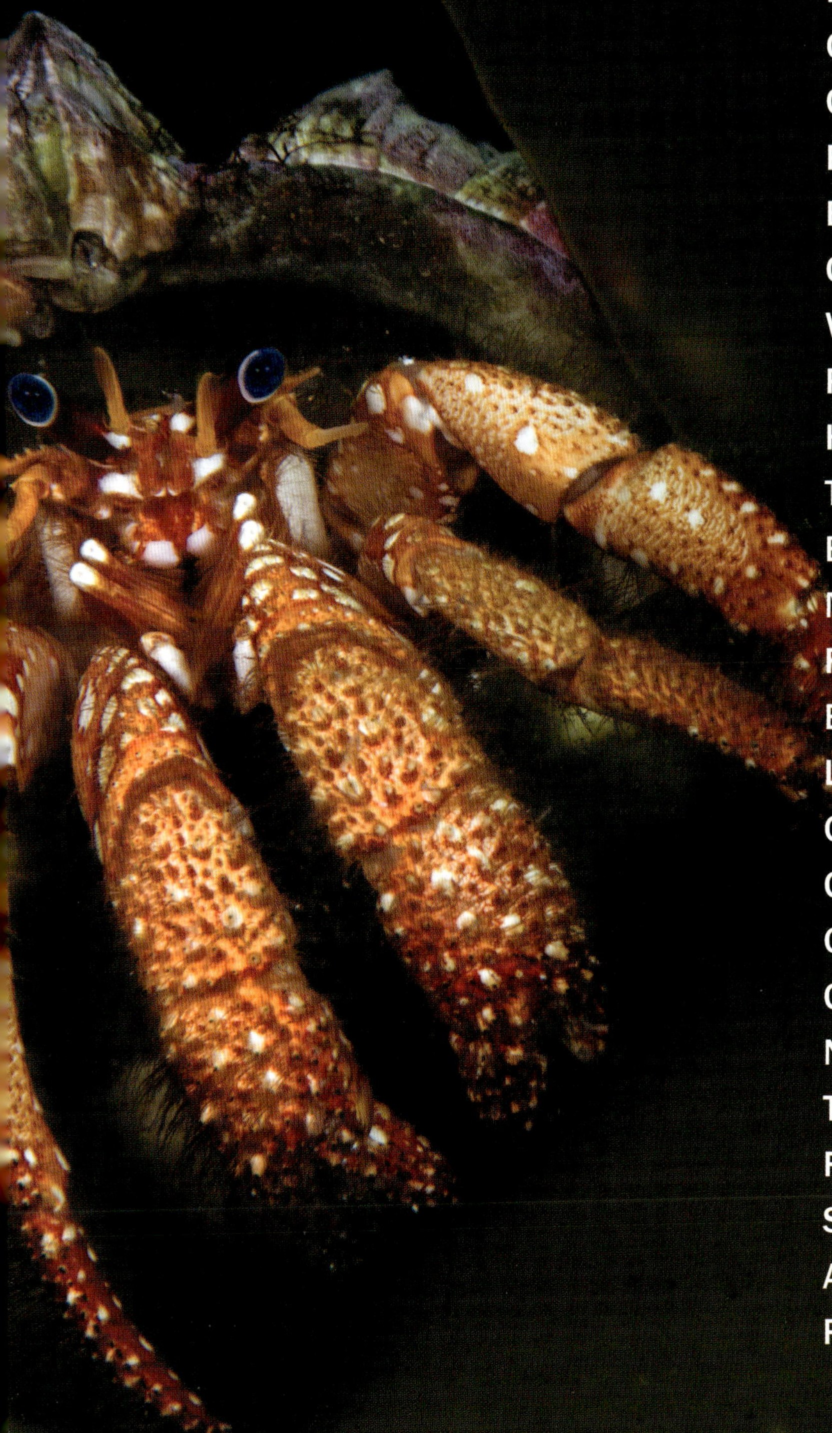

CONTENTS

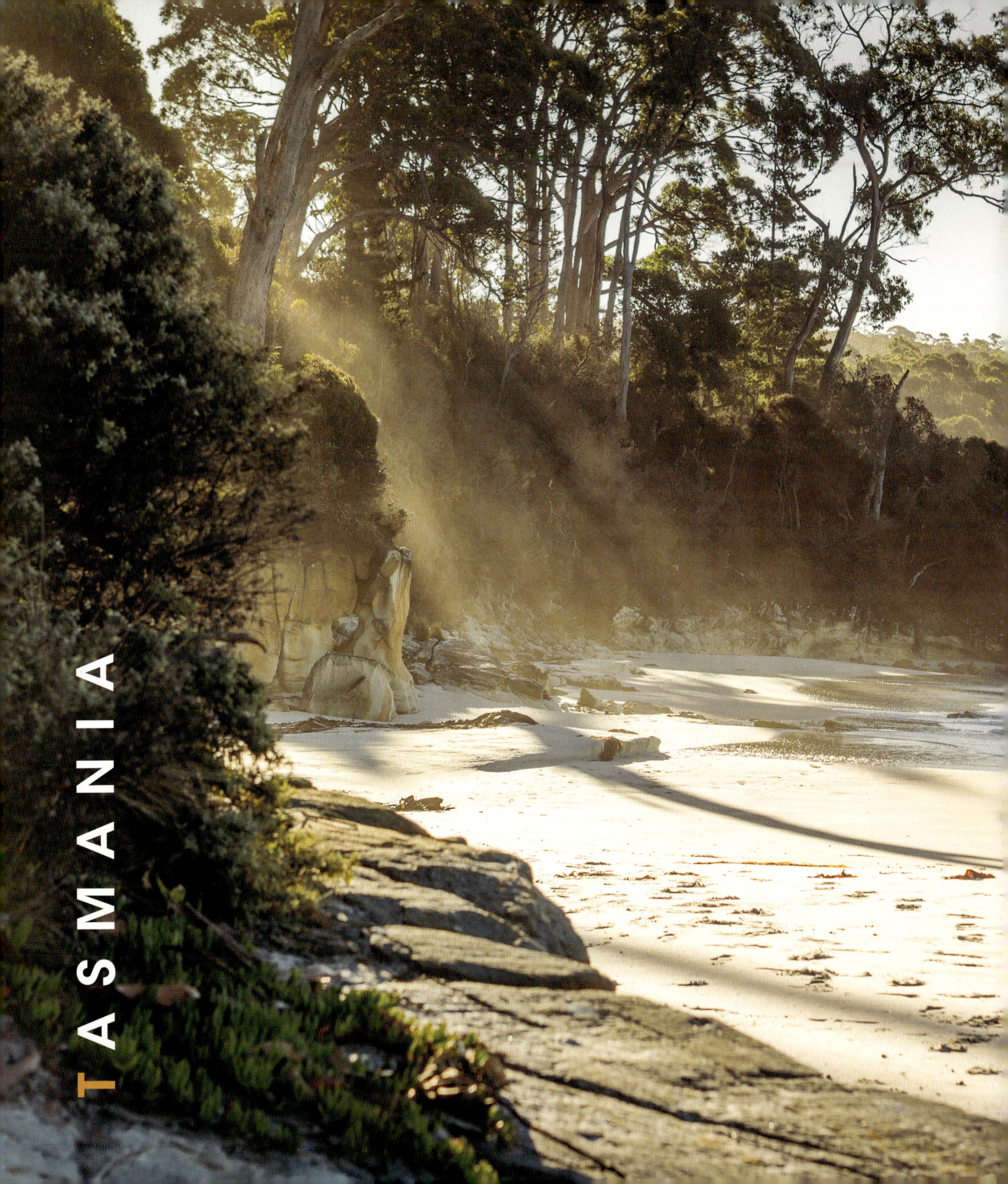
TASMANIA

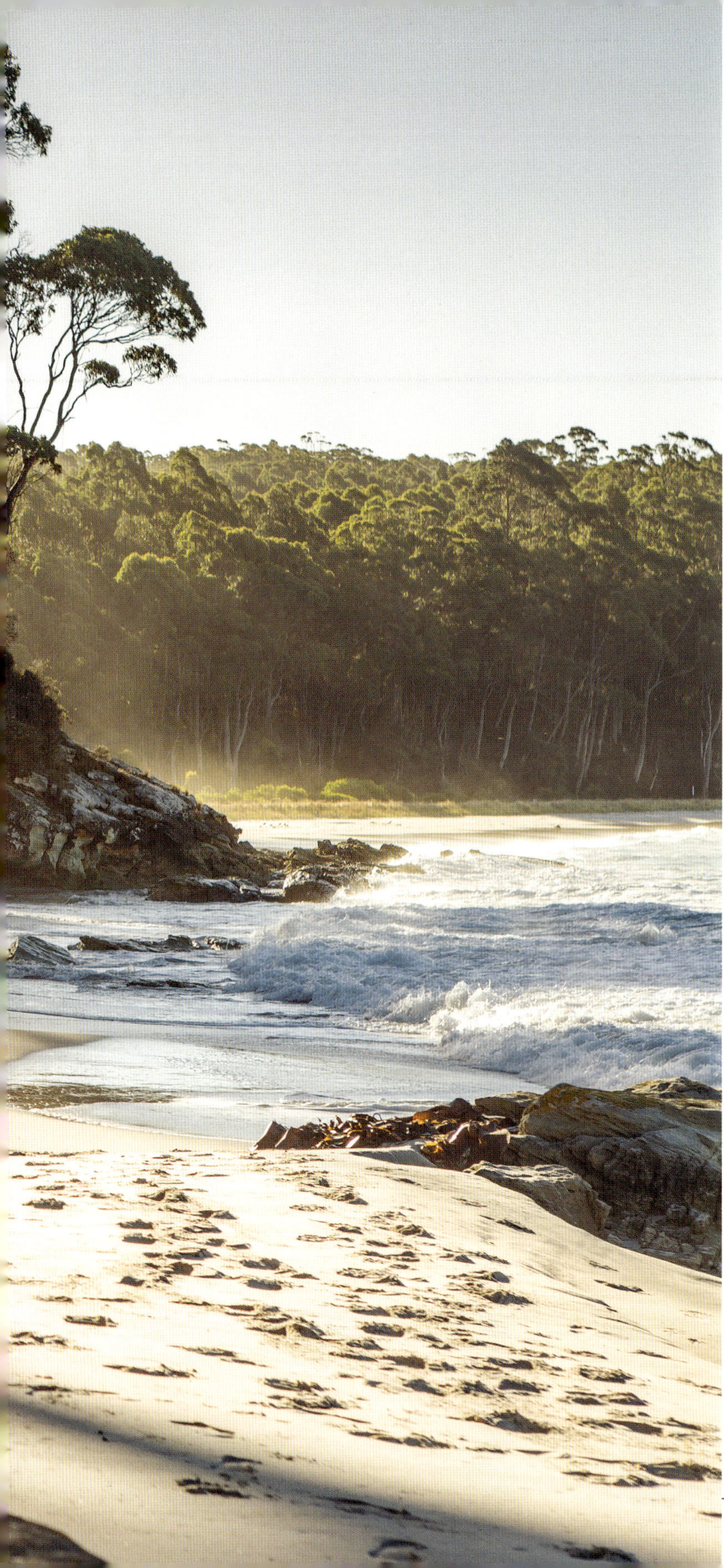

This heart-shaped island state, about the size of Ireland, is often left off maps and itineraries. In this unique part of Australia there are no vast shimmering plains, no red dusty interior, no searing heat or enormous distances to travel. Instead, much of the island is a magnificent wilderness, covered in mountains and rainforest, bordered by a dramatic coastline of cliffs and meandering peninsulas. More than a third of Tasmania is protected by a World Heritage Area, national parks and forest reserves. The cleanest air and sea in the world, swathes of uninhabited, untouched land and a tiny population attract visitors seeking tranquil, natural beauty. Tasmania's isolation has also helped preserve many species of wildlife and flora that are now extinct on the mainland. It's a place made for adventure where almost every outdoor activity is possible, from rock climbing and kayaking to diving and bushwalking. Of course there are more sedate pleasures too – driving wonderful scenic routes, tasting the island's superb food and wine, and exploring the ruins of Tasmania's colonial past. It's a place where you can experience some of the world's truly wild country and choose whether to challenge yourself to your very limits or simply savour this island jewel in the greatest of comfort.

■ Left : The beach at Resolution Creek in Adventure Bay, Bruny Island. Tasmania's east coast beaches are gentle and sunny with big round boulders splashed with orange lichen while its west coast beaches are craggy, brooding and wild.

TASMANIA

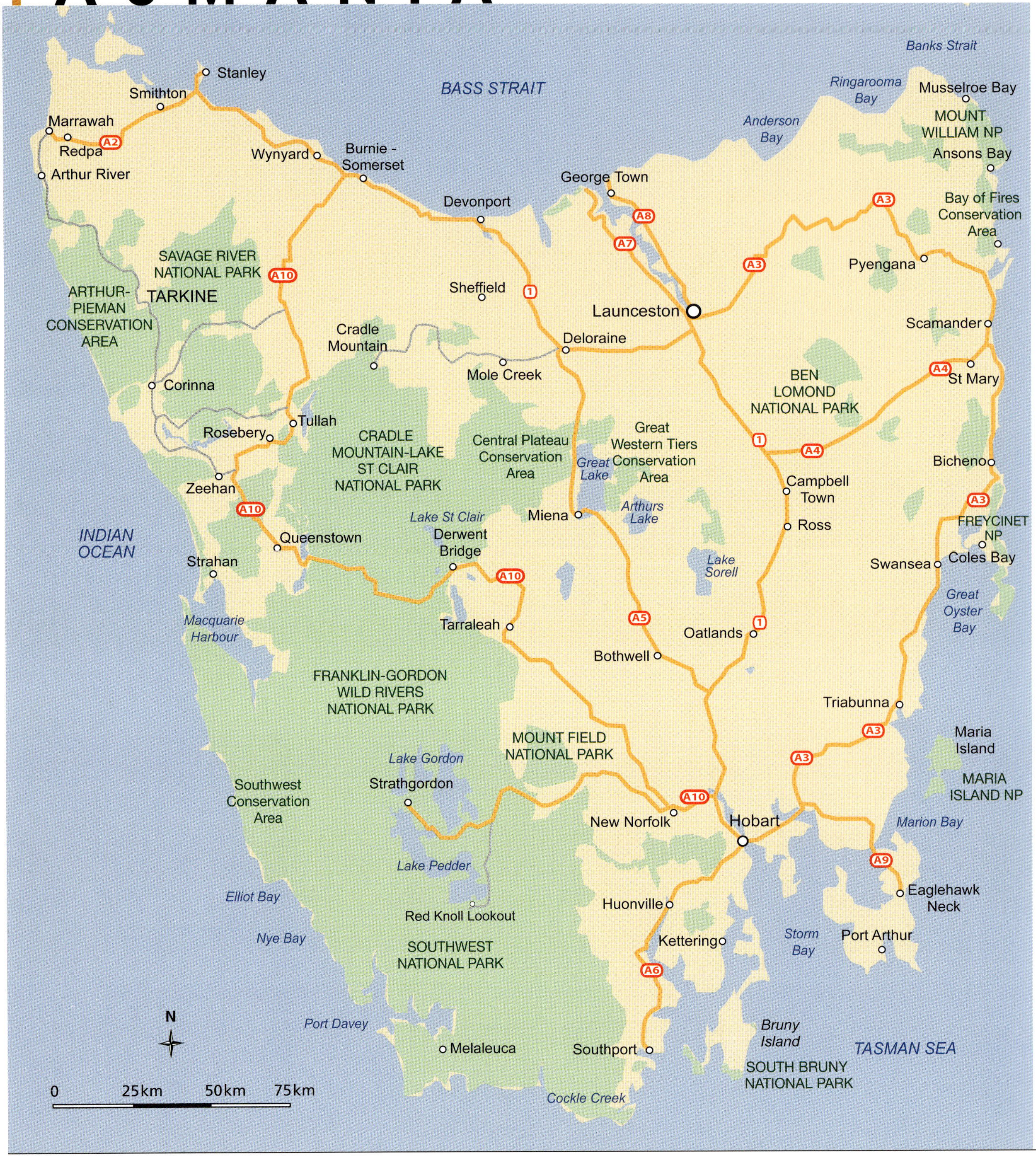

Banks Strait
BASS STRAIT
Stanley
Smithton
Marrawah
Redpa
A2
Arthur River
Wynyard
Burnie - Somerset
Devonport
George Town
Ringarooma Bay
Musselroe Bay
MOUNT WILLIAM NP
Anderson Bay
Ansons Bay
Bay of Fires Conservation Area
A3
A8
A7
A10
SAVAGE RIVER NATIONAL PARK
TARKINE
ARTHUR-PIEMAN CONSERVATION AREA
Sheffield
Launceston
Pyengana
Scamander
Cradle Mountain
Deloraine
Mole Creek
BEN LOMOND NATIONAL PARK
A4
St Mary
Corinna
Tullah
Rosebery
CRADLE MOUNTAIN-LAKE ST CLAIR NATIONAL PARK
Central Plateau Conservation Area
Great Western Tiers Conservation Area
Great Lake
Bicheno
Zeehan
Campbell Town
Arthurs Lake
Miena
Lake St Clair
Ross
FREYCINET NP
INDIAN OCEAN
Queenstown
Derwent Bridge
Coles Bay
Swansea
Strahan
Lake Sorell
Macquarie Harbour
Tarraleah
A5
Oatlands
Great Oyster Bay
Bothwell
FRANKLIN-GORDON WILD RIVERS NATIONAL PARK
Triabunna
MOUNT FIELD NATIONAL PARK
Maria Island
Lake Gordon
MARIA ISLAND NP
Southwest Conservation Area
Strathgordon
New Norfolk
Hobart
Marion Bay
Lake Pedder
A9
Elliot Bay
Red Knoll Lookout
Huonville
Eaglehawk Neck
Nye Bay
SOUTHWEST NATIONAL PARK
Kettering
Storm Bay
Port Arthur
A6
N
Port Davey
Bruny Island
Melaleuca
Southport
TASMAN SEA
SOUTH BRUNY NATIONAL PARK
0
25km
50km
75km
Cockle Creek

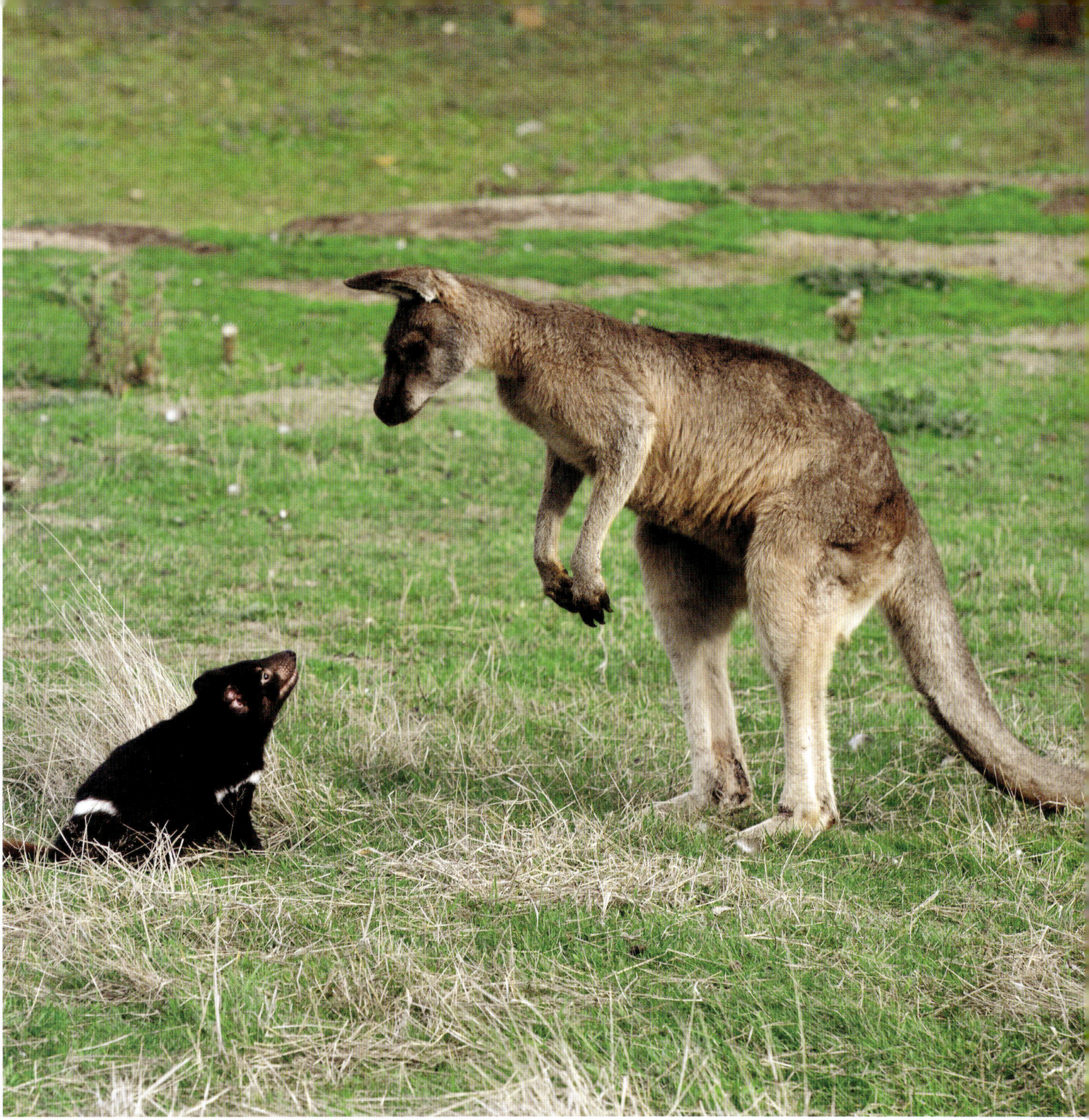

■ Above: In Tasmania wildlife encounters can be surprising. Tasmanian devils are usually nocturnal.

GEOLOGY

One of the most striking things about Tasmania is the diversity and dominance of its rock types. This is not the Australia that people imagine, with its vast dry plains and ranges weathered down by the eons into low ridges. It's a dramatic landscape with distinctive spiky mountain ranges and thousands of small lakes ground into the highlands by glaciers. Some of the oldest rocks in Tasmania are quartzites and schists that were once sediments in a shallow sea. They can now be seen in the west, such as Frenchmans Cap and the Arthur Ranges. The granite of the east coast's Freycinet Peninsula and Bay of Fires, is cooled magma from the time of the collision of two tectonic plates in the Devonian period that formed the Great Dividing Range in eastern Australia. Later, in the Jurassic period 200 million years ago, molten rock forced through the earth's crust during the breakup of Gondwana solidified into the dolerite that so dominates Tasmania's landscape - with its soaring hexagonal columns and dark, brooding nature at Mount Wellington, Ben Lomond and the Tasman Peninsula.

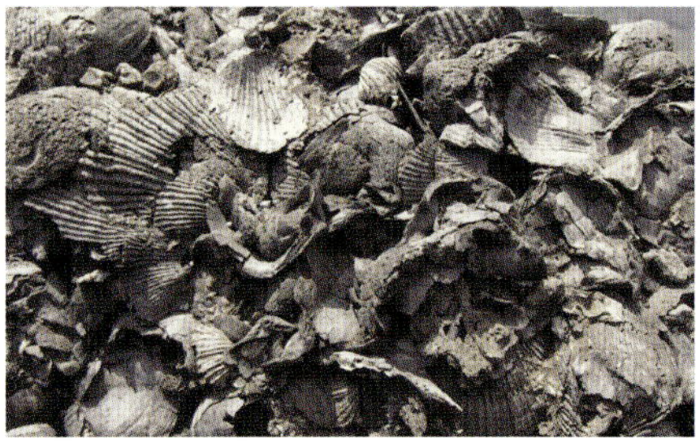

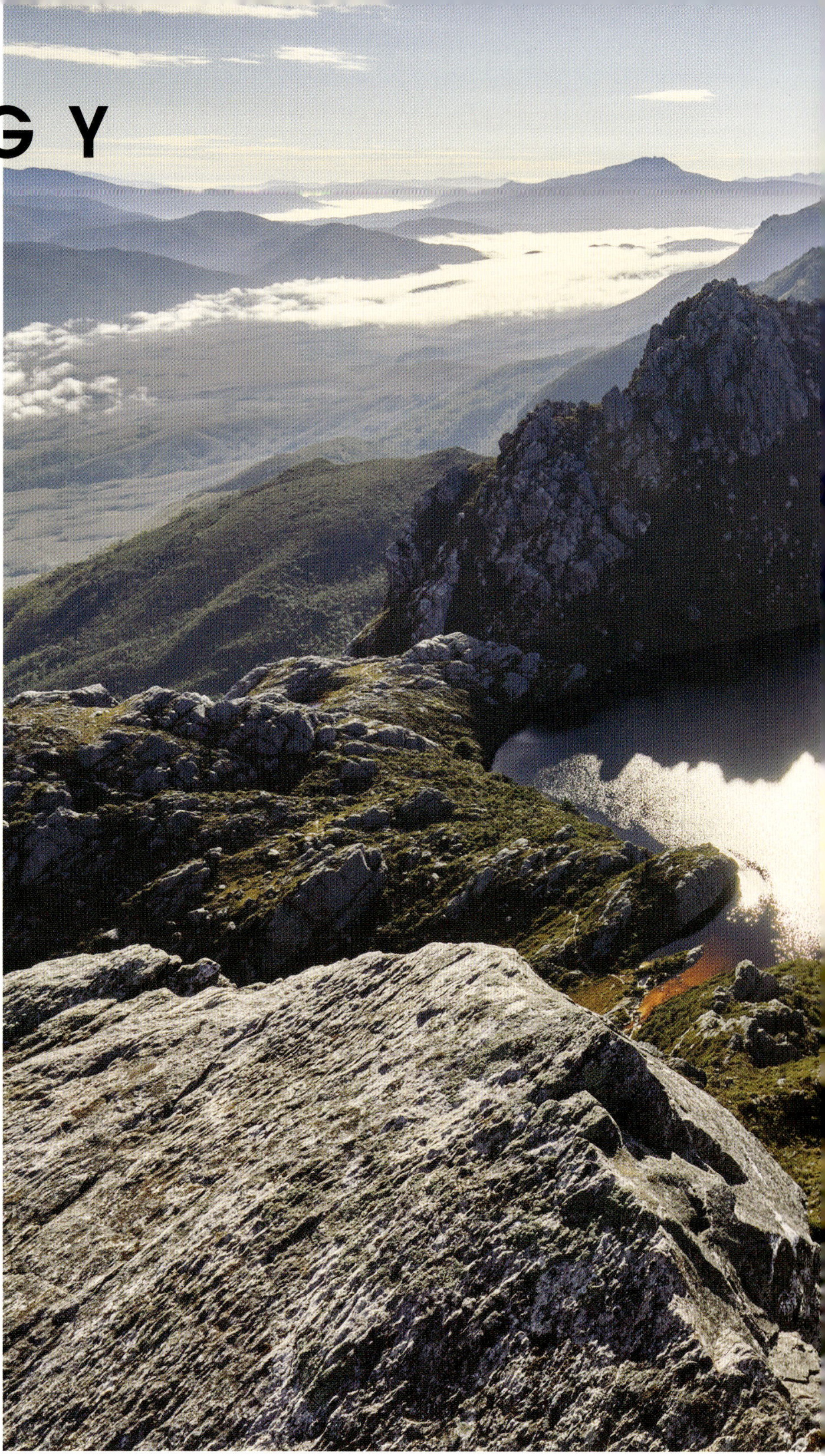

Above: Permian-era marine creatures at Maria Island's Fossil Cliffs.

Right: Lake Oberon in the early morning light, taken from the summit of Mount Sirius in the Western Arthur Range.

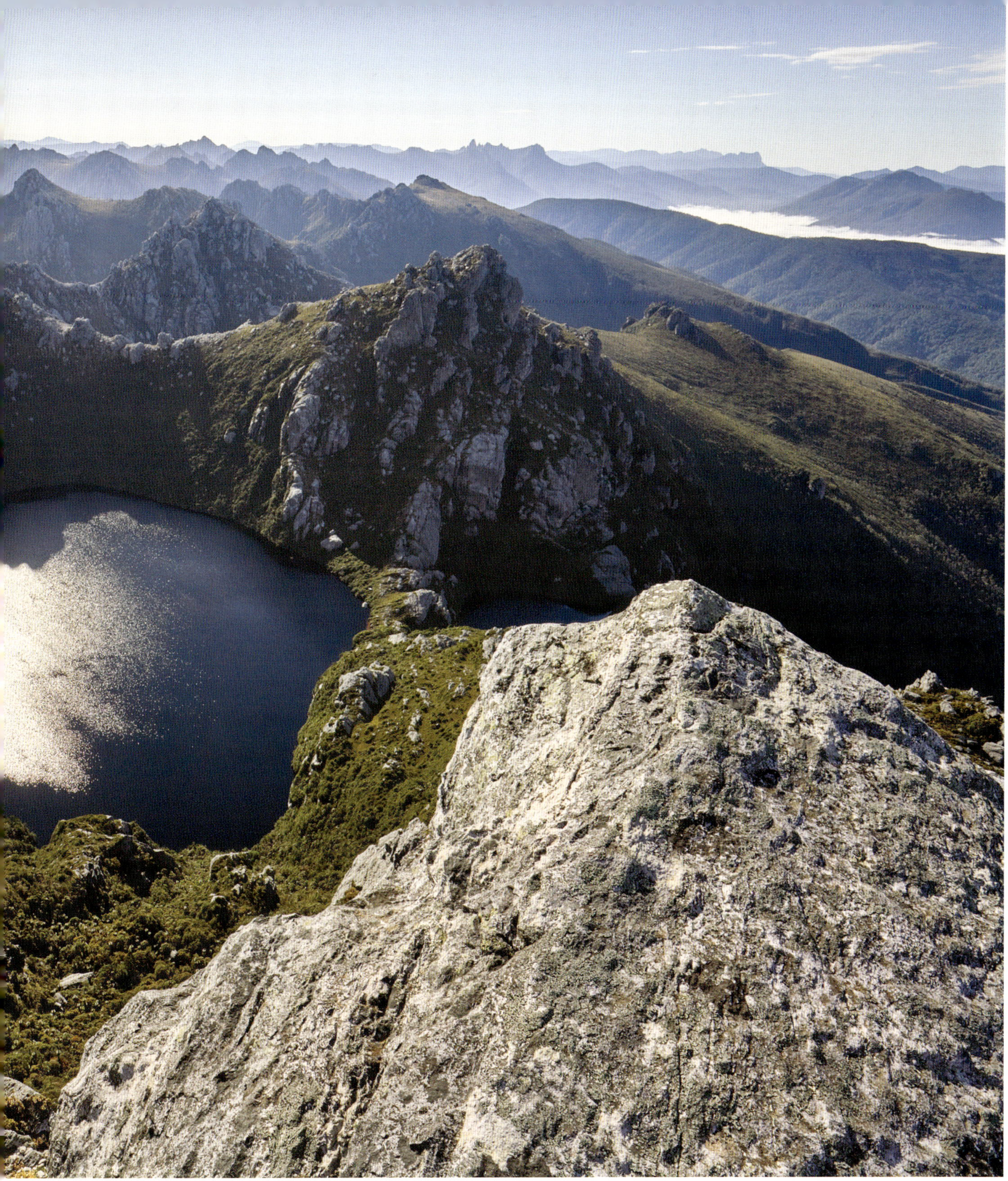

CLIMATE

The island state has a cool temperate climate and doesn't experience the extremely high temperatures that other states do. Even in summer it doesn't get much hotter than the low twenties. Generally the most comfortable months to visit are October to March, and some of the major walks and tours don't operate outside this period. Yet there are many delights to be enjoyed in winter too – not least the incredible food and wine, beautifully cosy accommodation, snowy mountain ranges and more! In fact, the only consistent thing about Tasmania's weather is its unpredictability. You can have four seasons in one day, snow in summer and sunny blue skies in winter. Rainfall varies dramatically across the island – the western half has an annual average of 2400 mm whereas the milder eastern half gets about 650 mm annually, with Hobart and the Midlands Highway area being a little drier. Right in the path of the 'roaring 40s' winds, it's best to be prepared for all conditions when you visit Tasmania, especially if you will be in alpine country or spending a lot of time outdoors. Warm layers and a waterproof jacket are essential and could even be life saving.

SUMMER

■ (December - February)
Peak season with temperatures ranging from 10-24° C. The best time to enjoy the state's stunning beaches with water temperatures at their warmest at 18° C.

AUTUMN

■ (March - May)
Lovely clear light and settled weather patterns are typical of Autumn here but the real highlight is the season's colour. Tasmania has many deciduous trees – Oaks, Ash, Elm and Poplar – but also the unique native deciduous beech or fagus which turns alpine country golden in April. Temperatures range from 5 to 22° C.

WINTER

■ (June – August),
Rug up and embrace winter when there is no better time to enjoy Tasmanian comfort food. Hobart celebrates the darkness with the DARK MOFO festival in June, and the Huon Valley hosts a Mid Winter Fest in July. Temperatures range from a chilly 2° C up to 14° C.

SPRING

■ (September to November)
Temperatures range from 6-19° C and, thanks to those deciduous trees, blossoms and bright green leaves are everywhere but the weather can be unpredictable. It's a good time for walking and trout fishing.

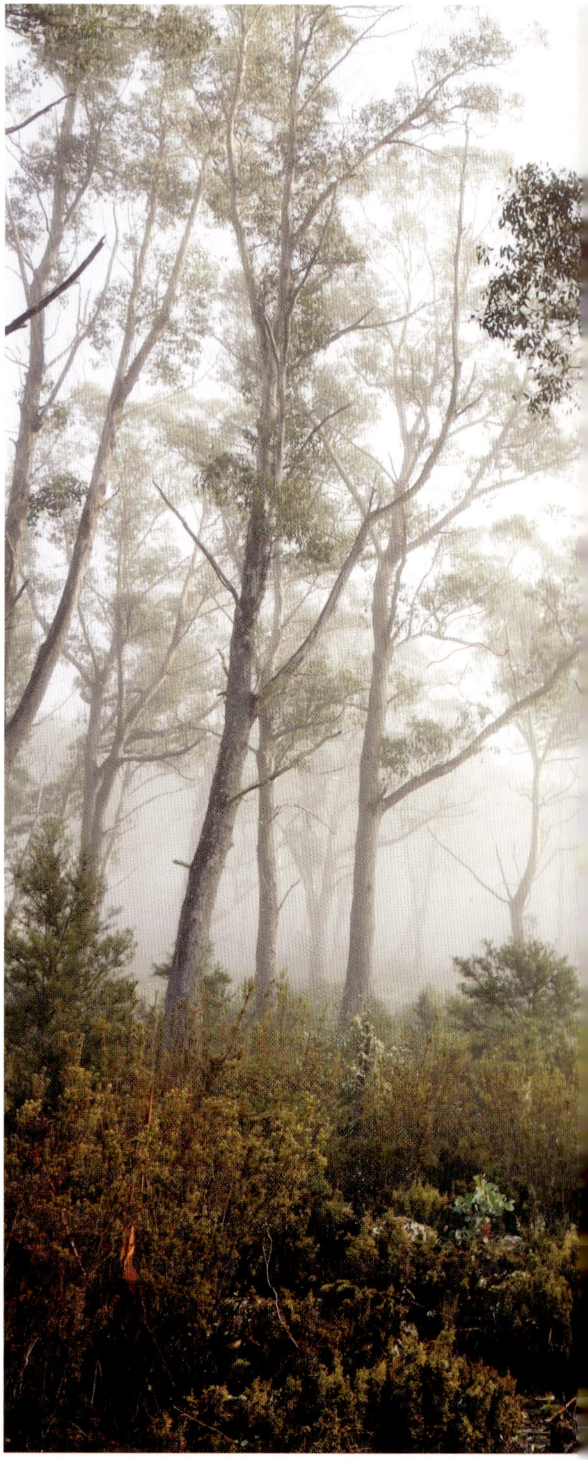

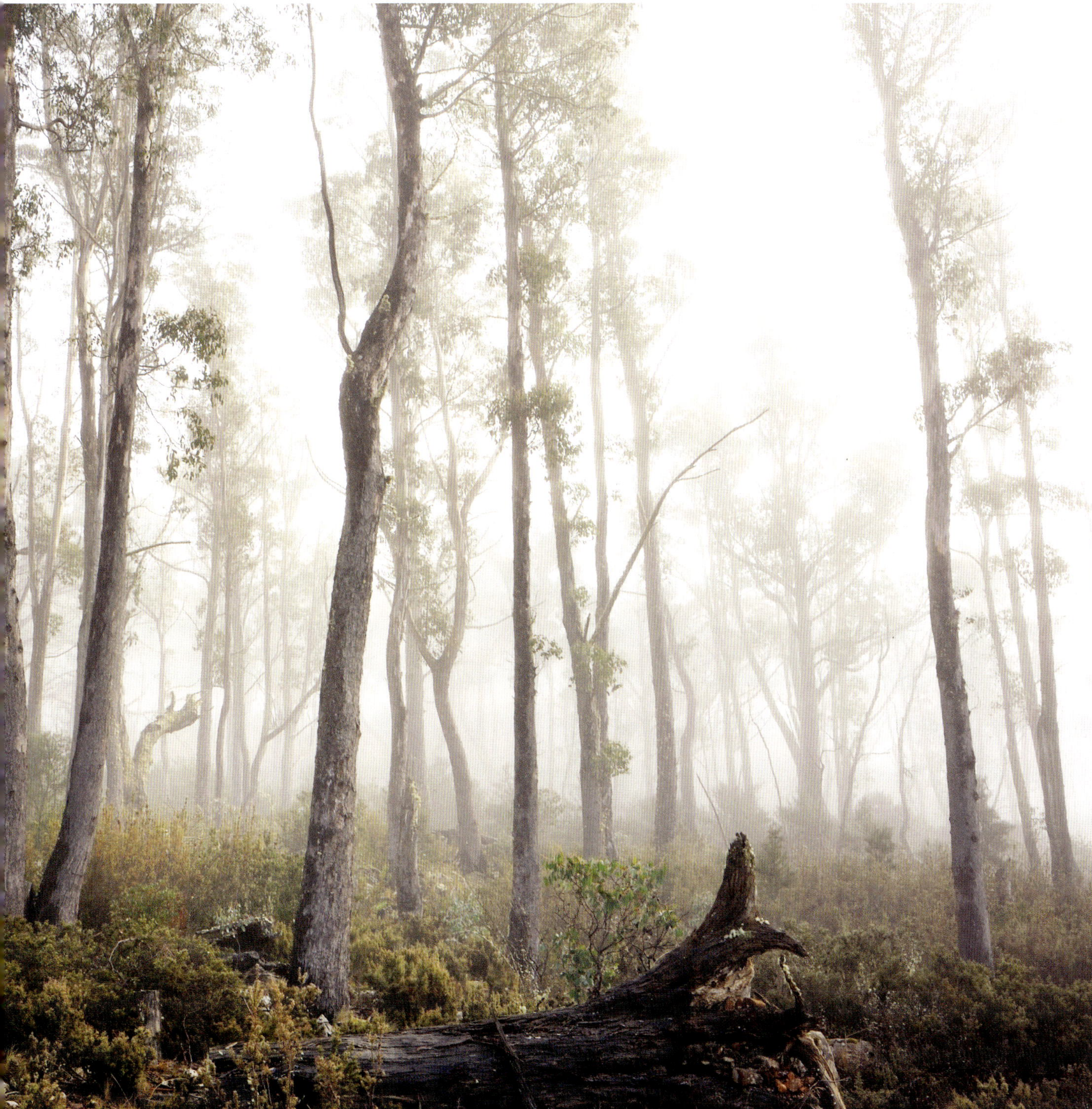

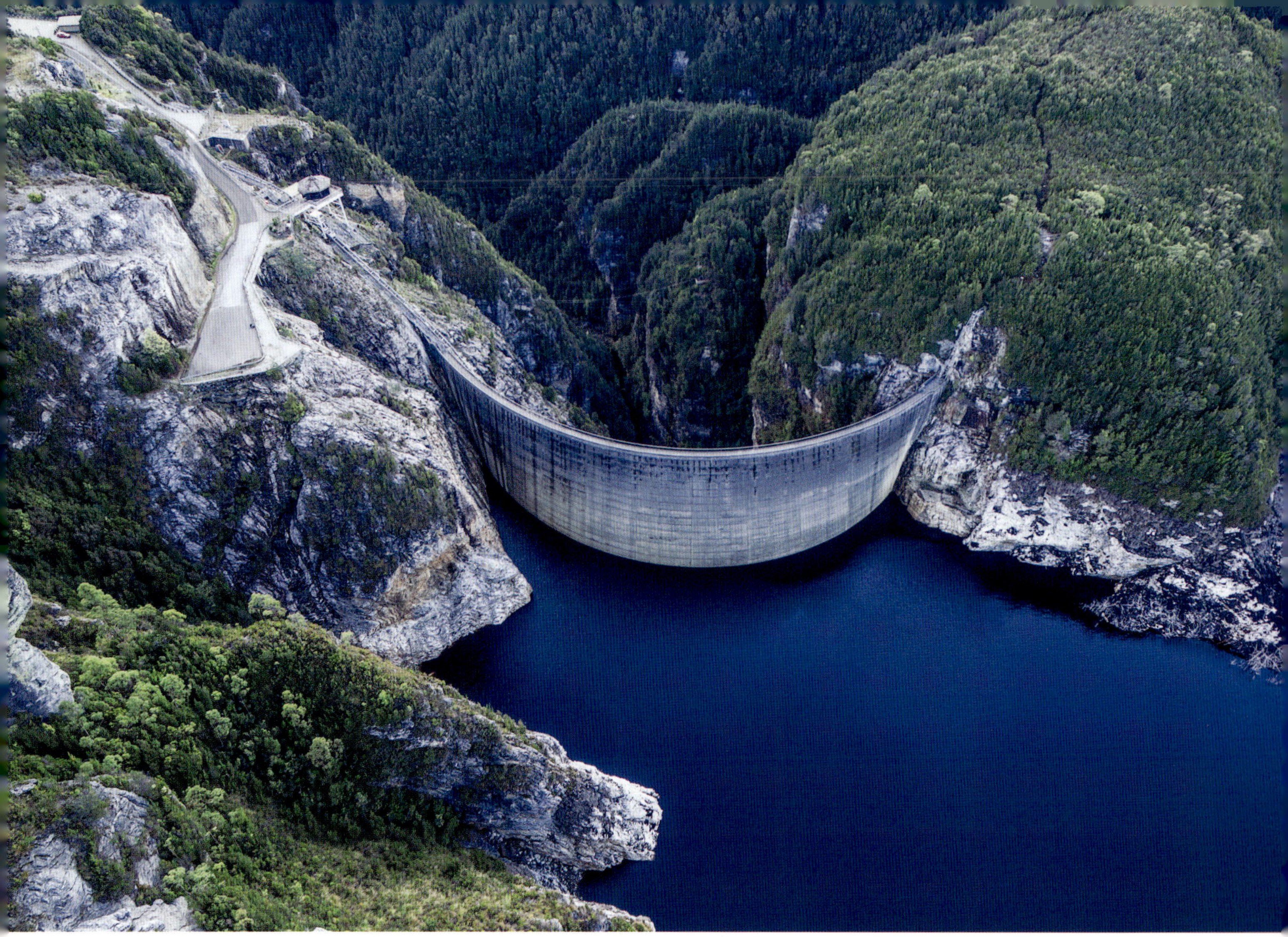

PEOPLE

People have lived in Tasmania for at least 40,000 years. During the last ice age when sea levels were low, Tasmania was not separated from the mainland. People and animals could travel back and forth across a land bridge from Wilson's Promontory in Victoria and northeast Tasmania. This land flooded about 12,000 years ago to become Bass Strait and Tasmania has been isolated ever since. By the time the British arrived in 1803, it is thought that there were nine tribes or nations, an estimated population of 3000-7000. Dutchman Abel Tasman was the first European to land on the island in 1642, which he named Van Diemen's Land after the Governor of the Dutch East Indies but it was renamed in his honour in 1856. A penal colony for its first four decades, the majority of Tasmania's population in the nineteenth century were convicts, ex-convicts or children of convicts. As Tasmanian society developed it remained devotedly British and loyalty to 'Home and Crown' underpinned its economic dependence on Britain. During the 1870s-1890s the state prospered as gold, tin and copper were found in the north and west. The government decided to produce hydroelectric power to support the new mining industry. Damning rivers and building power stations continued until the 1980s when conservationists succeeding in protecting some of the state's environmental treasures.

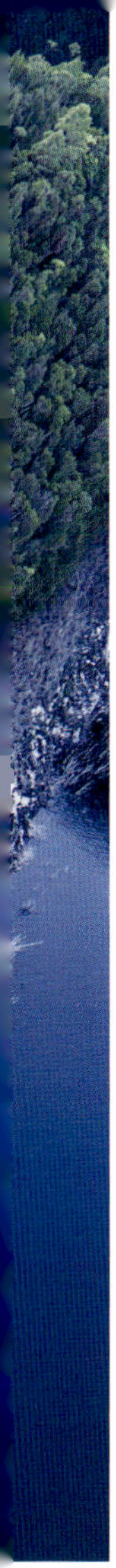

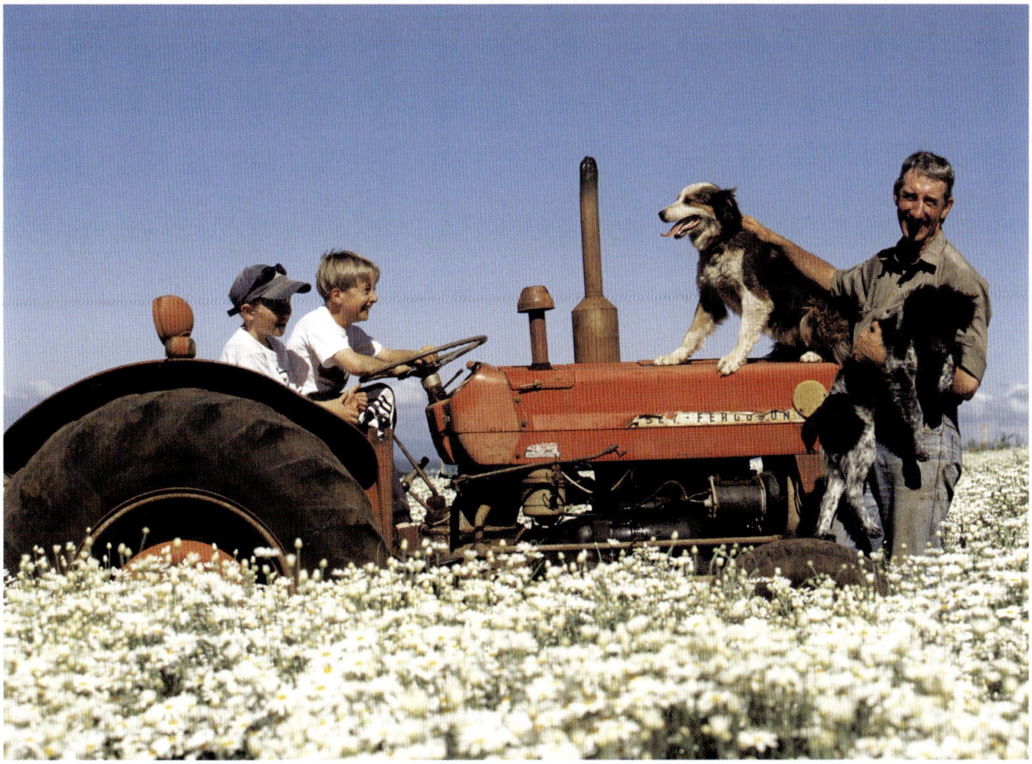

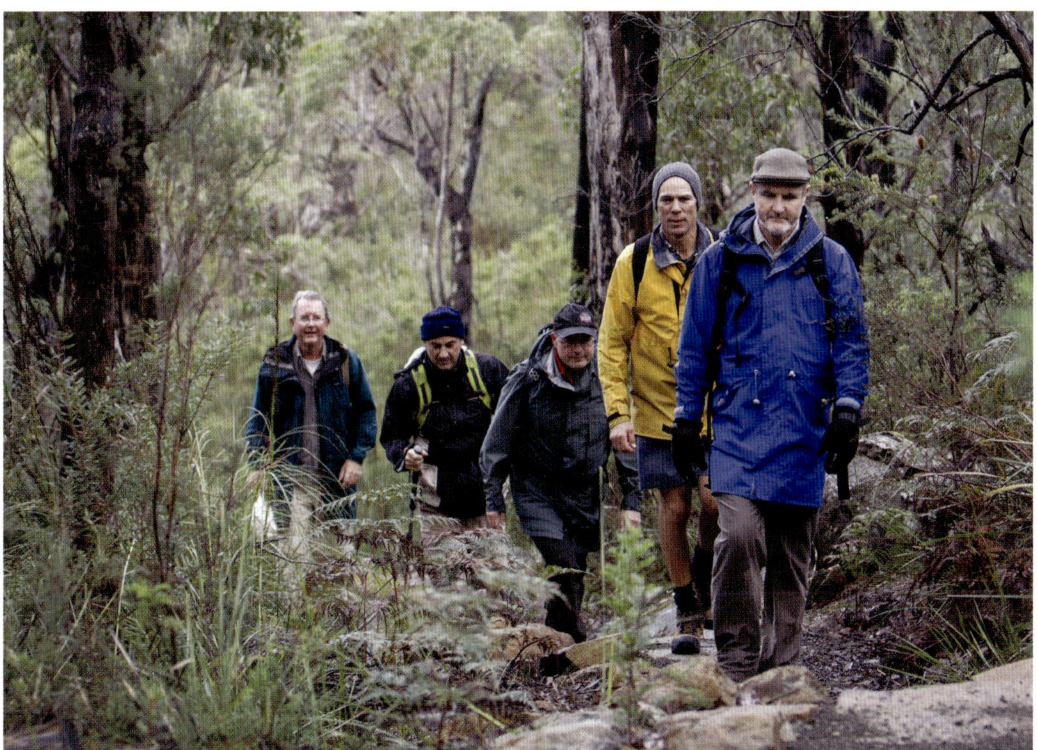

Far left: Gordon Dam near Strathgordon built in 1974. The power of landscape photography was demonstrated by Peter Dombrovskis famed 1979 photograph Morning Mist which played a pivotal role in halting construction of a similar dam in 1983, the Gordon-below-Franklin dam.

Top left: Farmer and family in a field of pyrethrum in fertile northern Tasmania.

Bottom left: Tasmanians are friendly, relaxed and resourceful. As an island people, they have a sense of being different and the deep attachment that comes from knowing a small place so well. They are also a divided people – between those who value jobs more than virgin forest and rivers, and others who want to preserve the environment.

ECONOMY

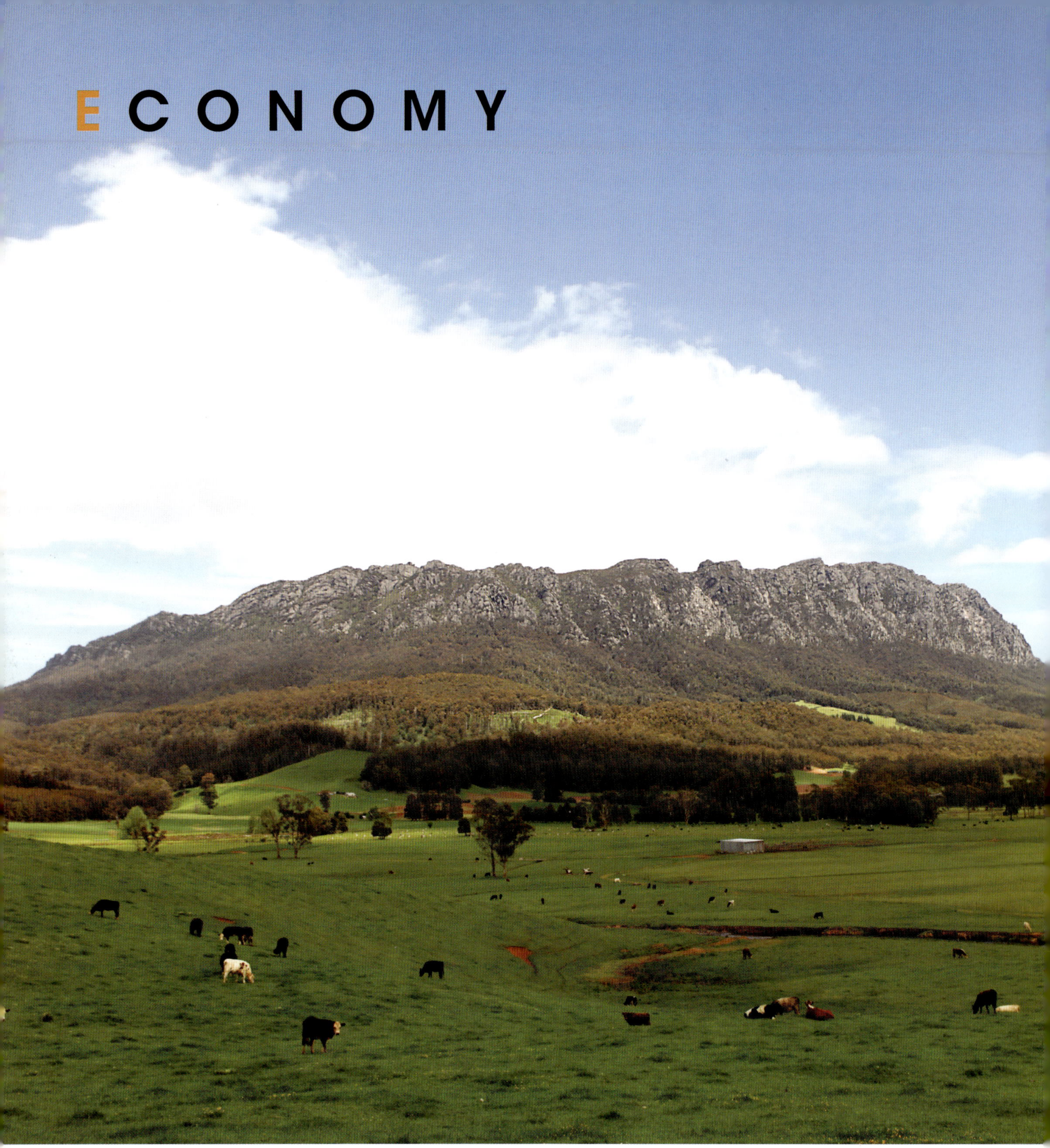

Tasmania covers 68,401 square kilometres, about the same size as Switzerland or Ireland, and has a population of 520,000. Just over half of Tasmanians live in Hobart or Launceston so outside these small liveable cities, you'll certainly be far from a crowd. The economy is mostly based on primary industries – agriculture, aquaculture, forestry and mining – but tourism is also a major industry contributing $1.4 billion (5% of the state's economy) to the state annually. In some areas, these industries are in conflict with each other. Many of Tasmania's 1.3 million visitors each year are drawn to Tasmania's pristine wilderness areas and wildlife yet some of these precious assets are threatened by logging, mining and even aquaculture. Balancing this conflict has long been a challenge for state governments but the economy is strong with a growing population drawn south by affordable housing. For visitors, the most enjoyable products of the state's economy are its superb food and beverages, created with pure air, rich soils and clean water. Seafood, honey, cheese, truffles, berries, apples, walnuts, and even saffron and wasabi, are prime Tasmanian products exported around the world. Pinot noir and sparkling wine, plus boutique whisky and gin distilleries, cider and beer are also highly prized.

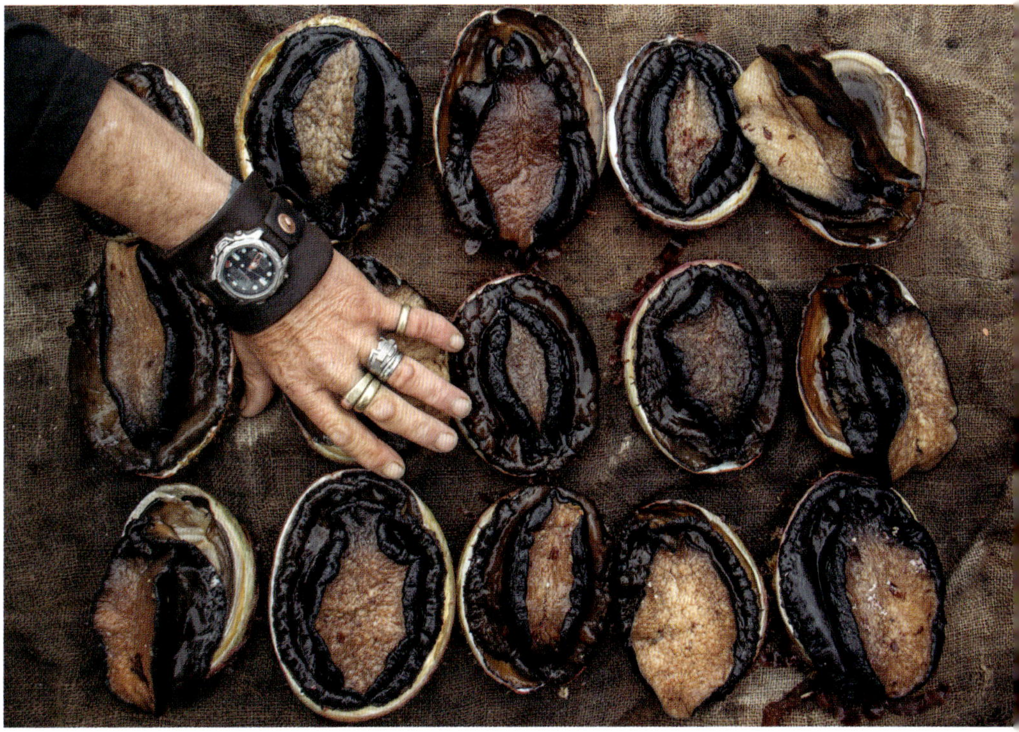

Above: Tasmania's abalone, oysters, crayfish and mussels are prized throughout Australia and exported worldwide. These black-lipped abalone were harvested off the Actaeon Islands in southern Tasmania. The state is also a major producer of farmed salmon and ocean trout in the D'Entrecasteaux Channel and Macquarie Harbour.

Left: The rich volcanic soil in northern Tasmania makes for prime agricultural land, like this farm below Mt Roland.

CULTURE

Tasmanian culture has a gloomy, gothic and brooding quality and this is partly due to the island's dramatic landscape and inclement weather but also because of its very dark history. Particularly the brutal horrors of the penal settlements of Macquarie Harbour and Port Arthur and the near-genocide of the island's indigenous population. Settled in 1803 by the British, the new colony became a place to banish the very worst of the convicts – those who had re-offended, absconded or threatened mutiny. If flogging, hunger, hard labour and solitary confinement weren't bad enough, there was no prospect of escape from the isolated penal stations – among those who tried were men who resorted to cannibalism and one who disguised himself in a kangaroo skin. For indigenous people, the first two decades of the nineteenth century were a time of violent conflict as they resisted being pushed off their land, abducted or killed by colonists who stocked the land with a million sheep. By 1828, the government had declared martial law, which meant Aborigines could legally be shot on sight. In 1830 Governor Arthur ordered the 'Black Line', an advancing front of 2000 men intended to drive Aboriginal people into the Tasman peninsula. By this time there were only about 300 indigenous Tasmanians left and they were forced into exile on Flinders Island where many died of disease and heartbreak.

Truganini from Bruny Island died in 1876 and was considered the 'last' Tasmanian Aboriginal. In fact, Aboriginal people survived on Tasmanian islands such as the Furneaux group off the north coast, descendants of indigenous women and European whalers and sealers. These people, known as Palawa, have had some success in recognition of identity and sacred sites, obtaining land rights, and the return of ancestors' bones from museum collections.

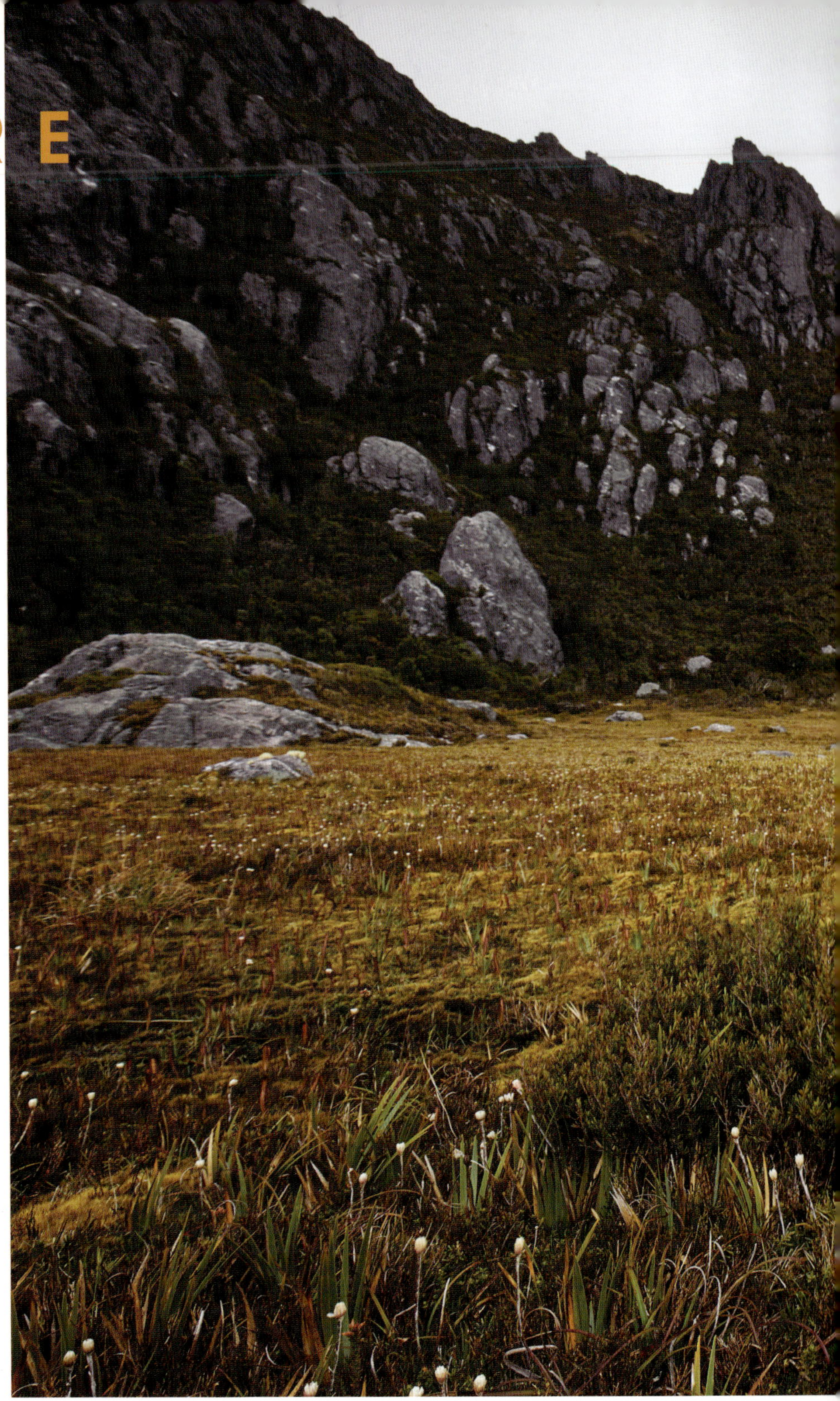

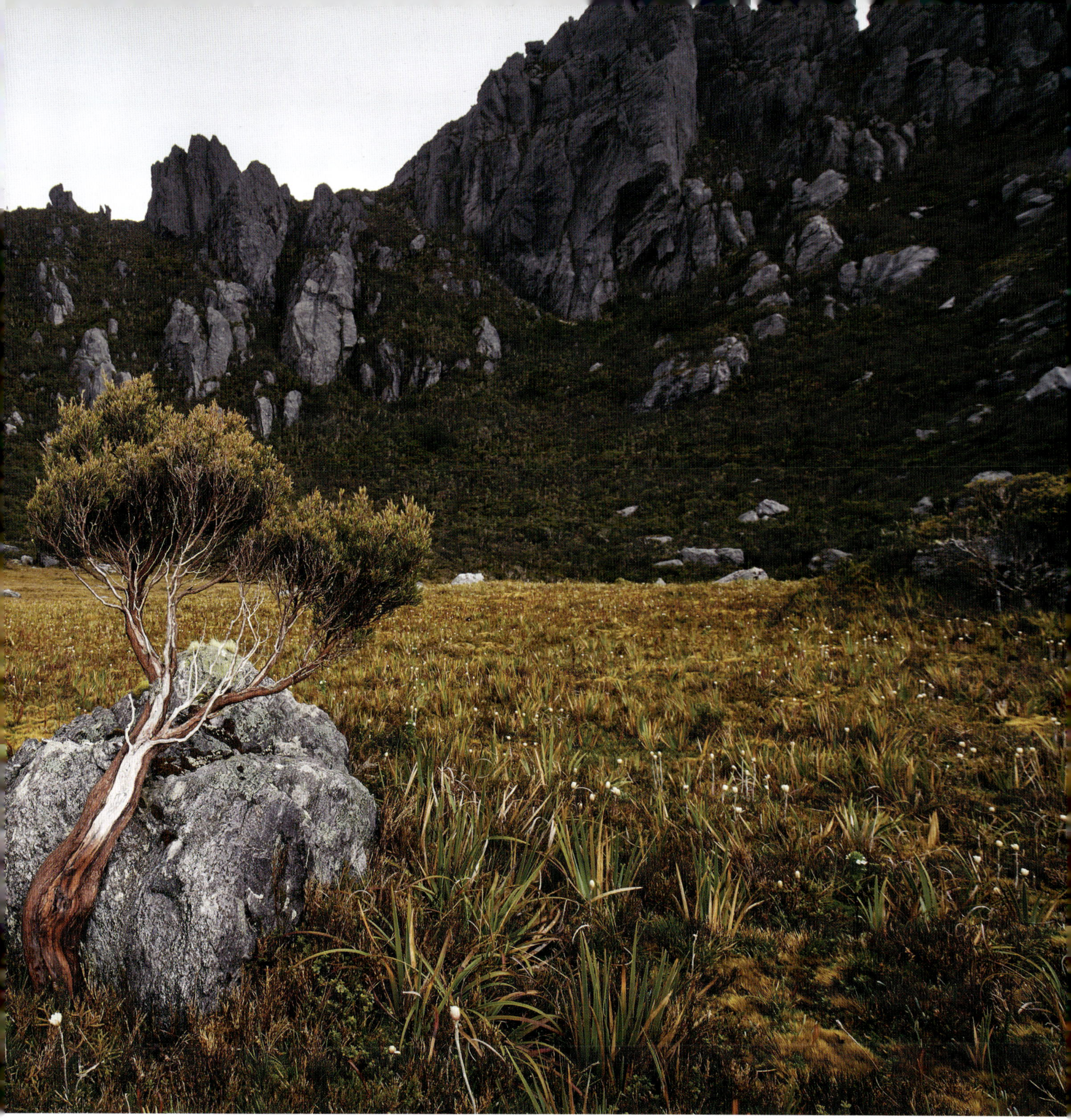

Right: All Tasmanian life is shaped by the elements like this tree and mountain range near Lake Oberon in the Western Arthur Range.

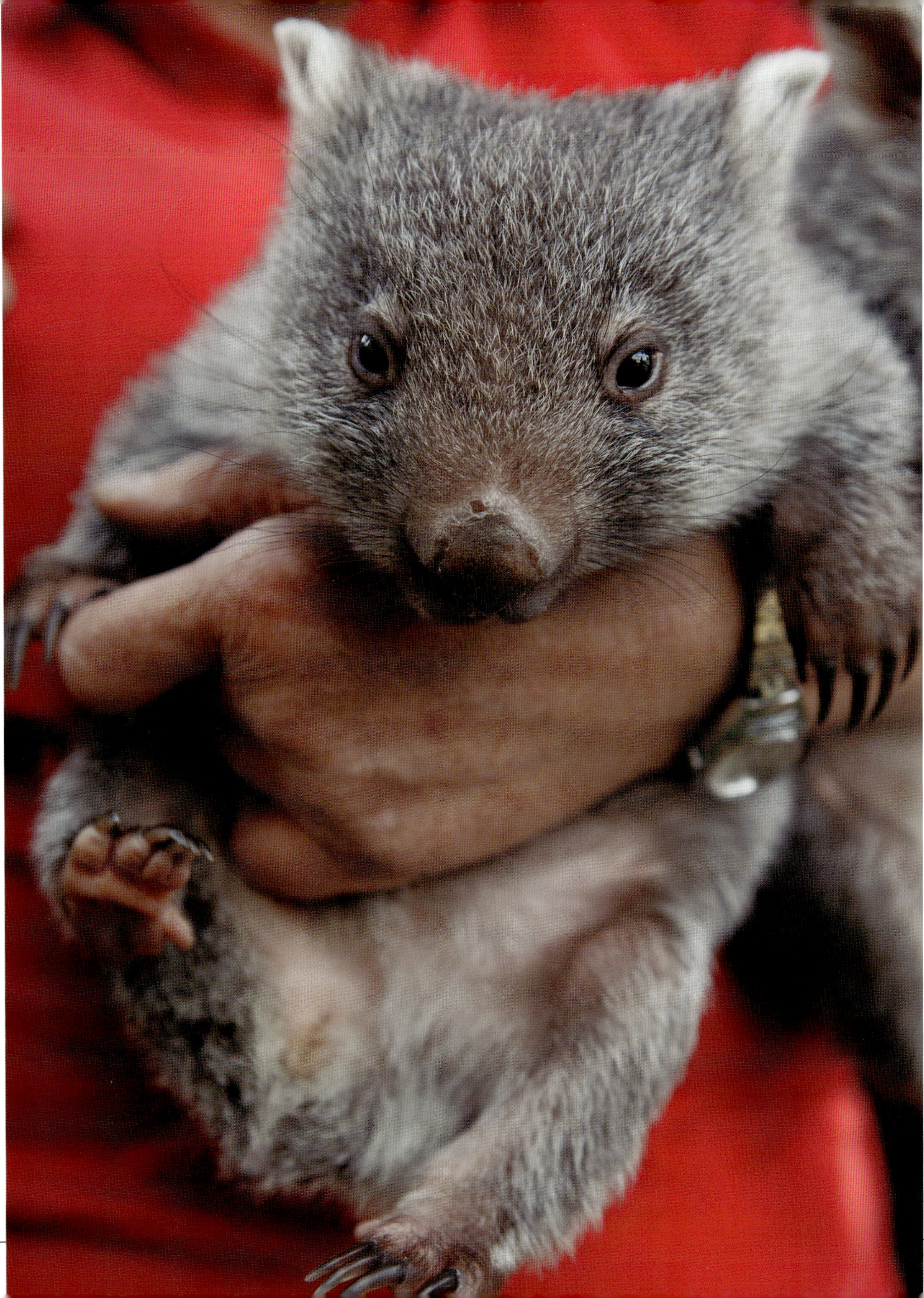

Isolated for 12,000 years, Tasmania's wildlife has adapted to the island's cool temperatures and plentiful rainfall. Wombats have thicker fur and echidna have fewer spines. Platypus are three times bigger than their mainland brothers and stroll between rivers in daylight, thanks to Tasmania's lack of large predators. The island has also protected creatures that are now extinct on the mainland, such as the Thylacine, the Tasmanian Devil, and the Eastern Quoll. It's an extraordinary place to see wildlife. Though devils and quolls are nocturnal, wombats, kangaroos, wallabies and pademelons are easily seen grazing in the morning or late afternoon on grasslands such as those at Narawntapu and Mt William National Parks. Tasmania also has a wealth of bird species, especially coastal birds such as petrels, eagles, plovers, herons, hawks and albatross, and rare parrots such as the orange-bellied parrot and swift parrot. Sadly, one animal you won't see is the legendary Tasmanian tiger or Thylacine. This shy nocturnal creature looked like a large dog but had black stripes on its rump and a pouch like a kangaroo. Blamed for killing livestock, in 1888 the Tasmanian government introduced a bounty for dead thylacines. Over a period of 21 years the government paid 2184 bounties and the last known animal died in 1936.

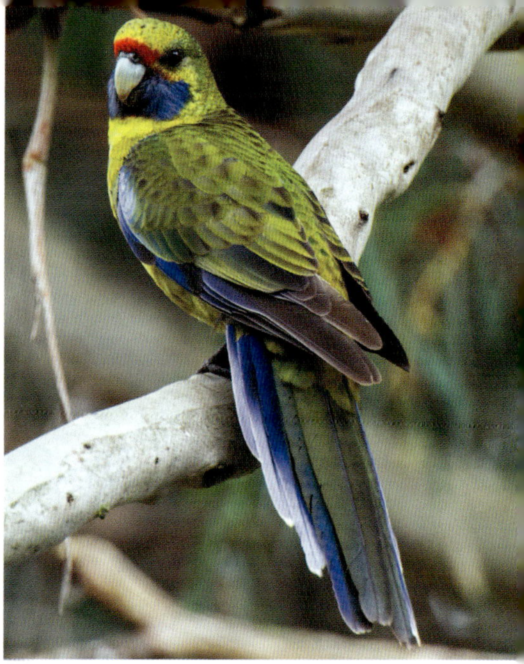

Opposite page: An orphan baby wombat, probably rescued from its mother's pouch by the roadside. Sadly many Tasmanian animals are killed by cars, especially at night. At this age they like to be cuddled but become less tactile when fully grown.

Above: Only found in Tasmania the common Green Rosella is Australia's largest rosella at 330-370 mm and lives in forests throughout the state.

Left: The short-beaked echidna has adapted to have more hair and fewer spines in Tasmania to keep it warm in the cool climate. The echidna and platypus are the world's only monotremes, or egg-laying mammals.

Below: Now extinct on the mainland, the cat-sized Eastern Quoll is a solitary nocturnal hunter living mostly on a diet of moths and grubs but it will also eat small mammals such as rabbits, mice and rats.

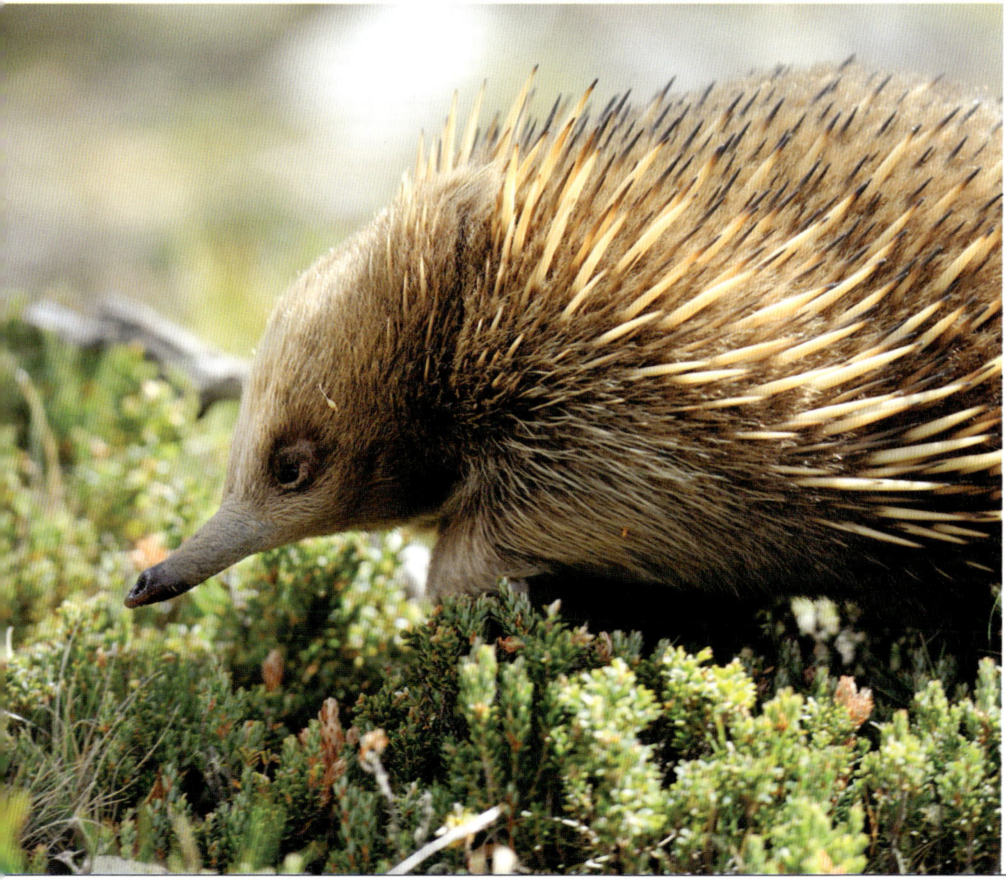

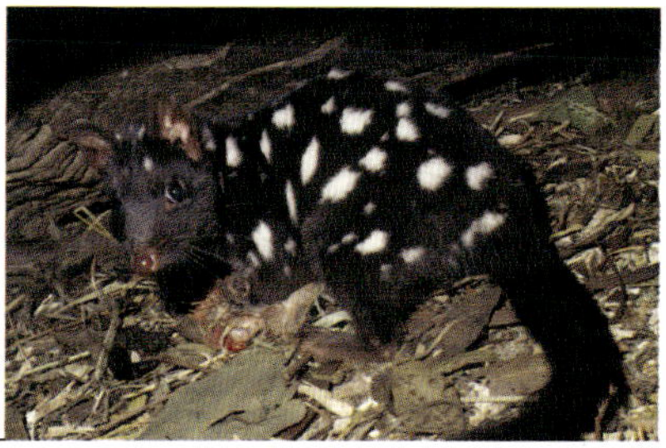

WILDLIFE

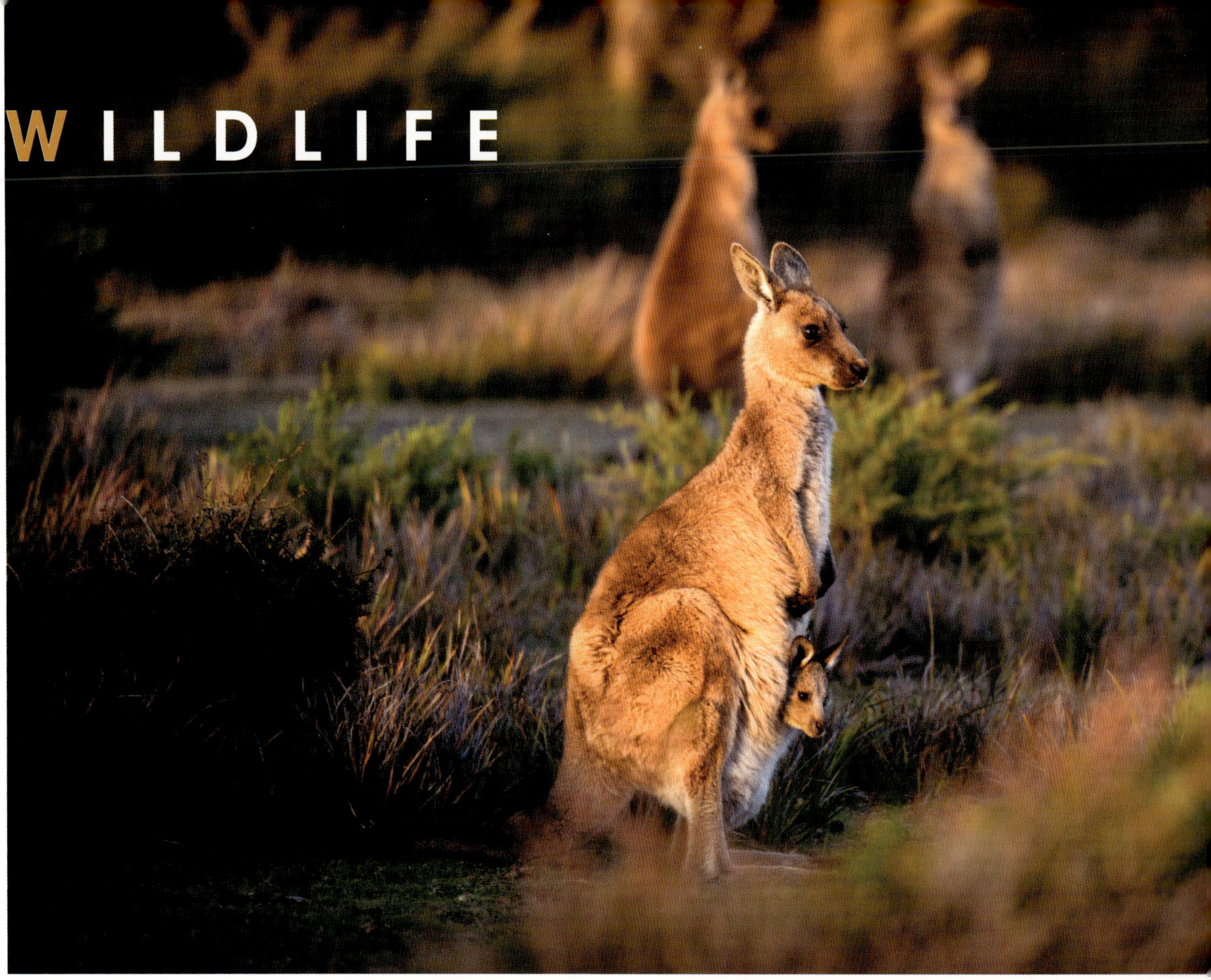

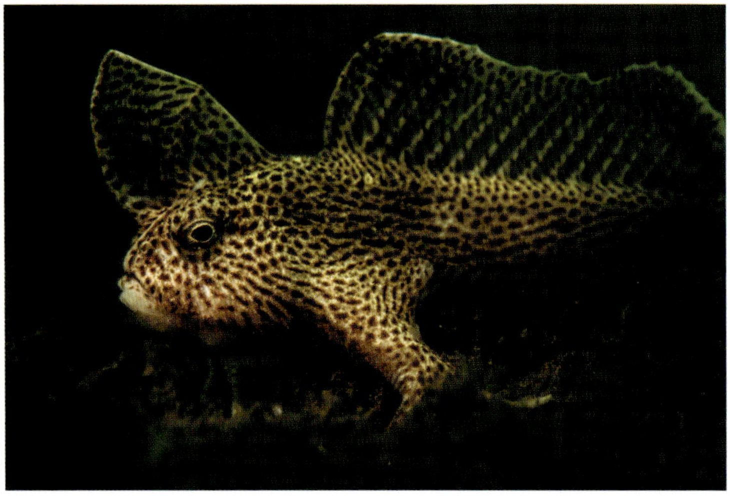

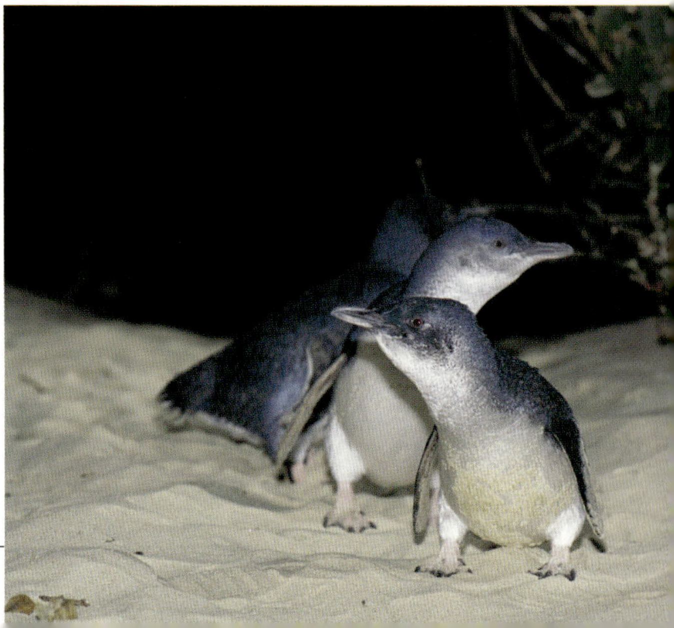

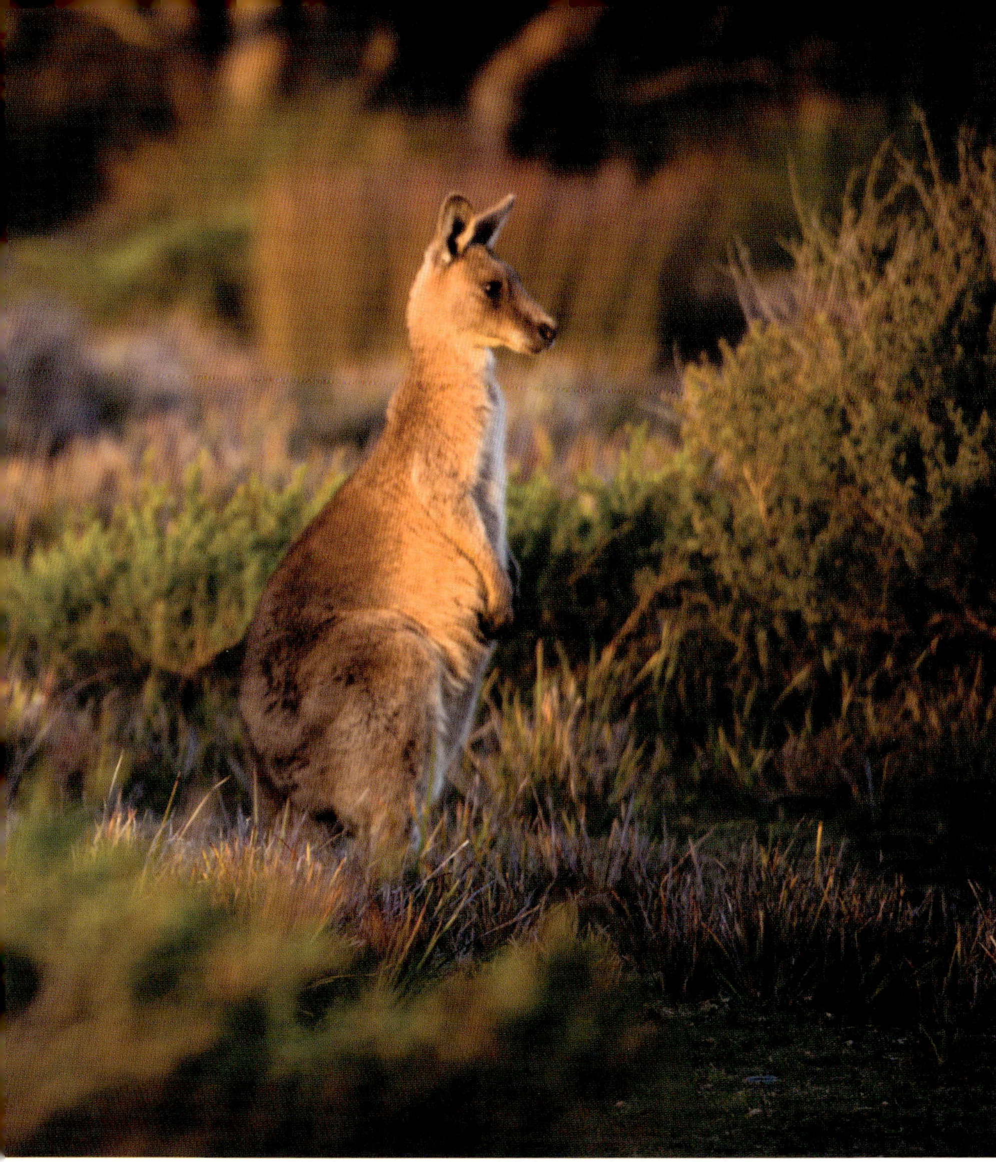

Left: Forester kangaroos in the Bay of Fires area where these is an excellent Aboriginal owned and operated guided walk, Wukalina Walk over 4 days.

Opposite page below: Tasmania's marine life is as extraordinary as its land bound cousins. It's estimated that 90 per cent of its marine species are found nowhere else on earth, including this Spotted handfish photographed in the Derwent River Estuary.

Far left: These little penguins wait for nightfall to leave the water on Bruny Island. At 33 cm they are the smallest species of penguin, and to escape predators they find safety in numbers as they dash to their burrows in the dunes. Spring is the best time to see them, on Bruny, Bicheno and towns on the north coast.

Left: Tasmanian devils live most of their lives alone but they will share a carcass. Despite the screaming and yowling as they tug at their prey, they will only defend the amount they need to eat. These scavengers have the most powerful bite relative to body size in the natural world and crunch through bone easily.

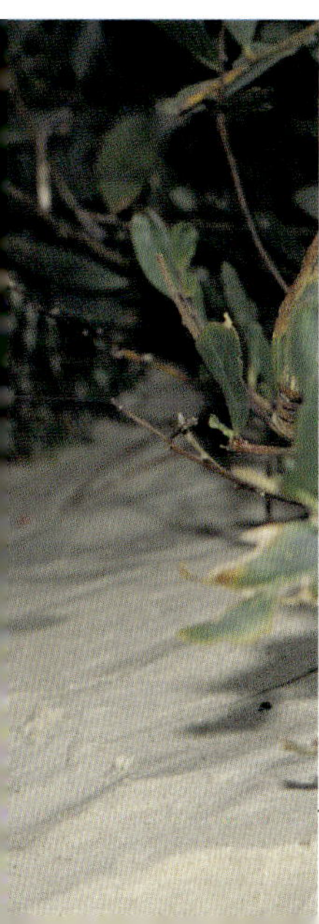

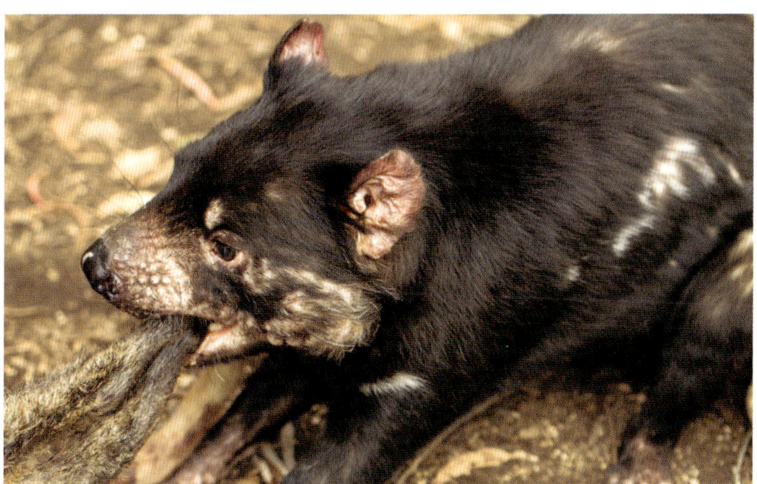

PLANTLIFE

As one of the last Gondwanan landmasses to separate from South America and Antarctica, just 45 million years ago, Tasmania carried a cargo of ancient plants which have survived due to its cool wet climate and isolation. Many of these special plants live in Tasmania's cool temperate rainforests, amid a carpet of mosses, lichen and colourful fungi. Here you'll find native conifers such as the Huon pine, King Billy pine, Celery-top pine and the Pencil pine. These trees grow very slowly but can live for more than a thousand years - some Huon pines have been dated to 3000 years old. Myrtle beech, sassafras and leatherwood are other uniquely Tasmanian rainforest species. Alpine areas are transformed in autumn by Australia's only deciduous tree, a beech known as fagus. The tiny ridged leaves of this tangled little tree turn golden in late April. Another Gondwanan remnant and spectacular resident of alpine country is the Pandani, the largest heath plant in the world. In western Tasmania, Buttongrass moorland dominates sodden plains with poor soil, whereas the drier eastern half of the state supports tussock and kangaroo grasslands, and coastal vegetation including banksia, manuka, paperbark and heathlands.

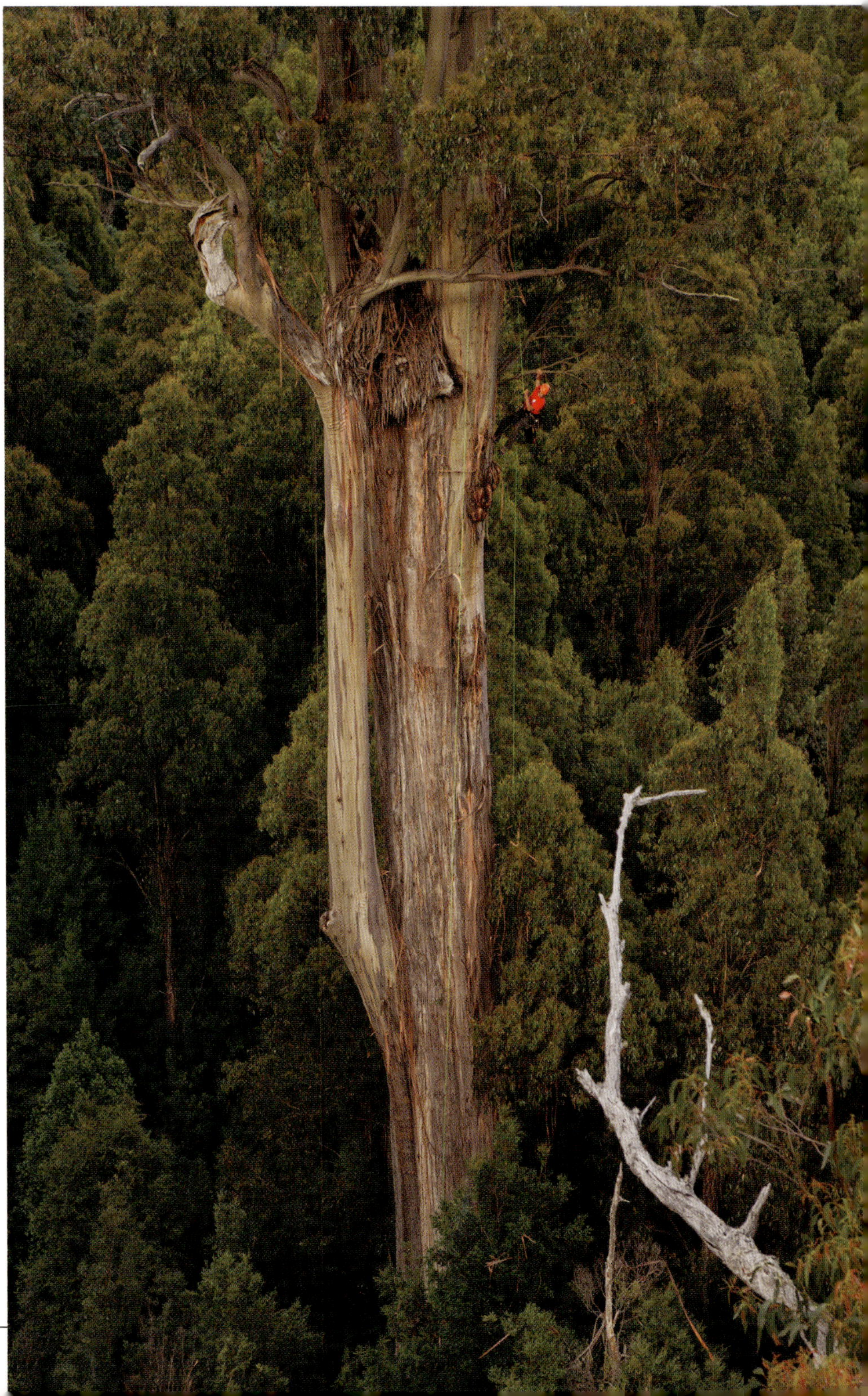

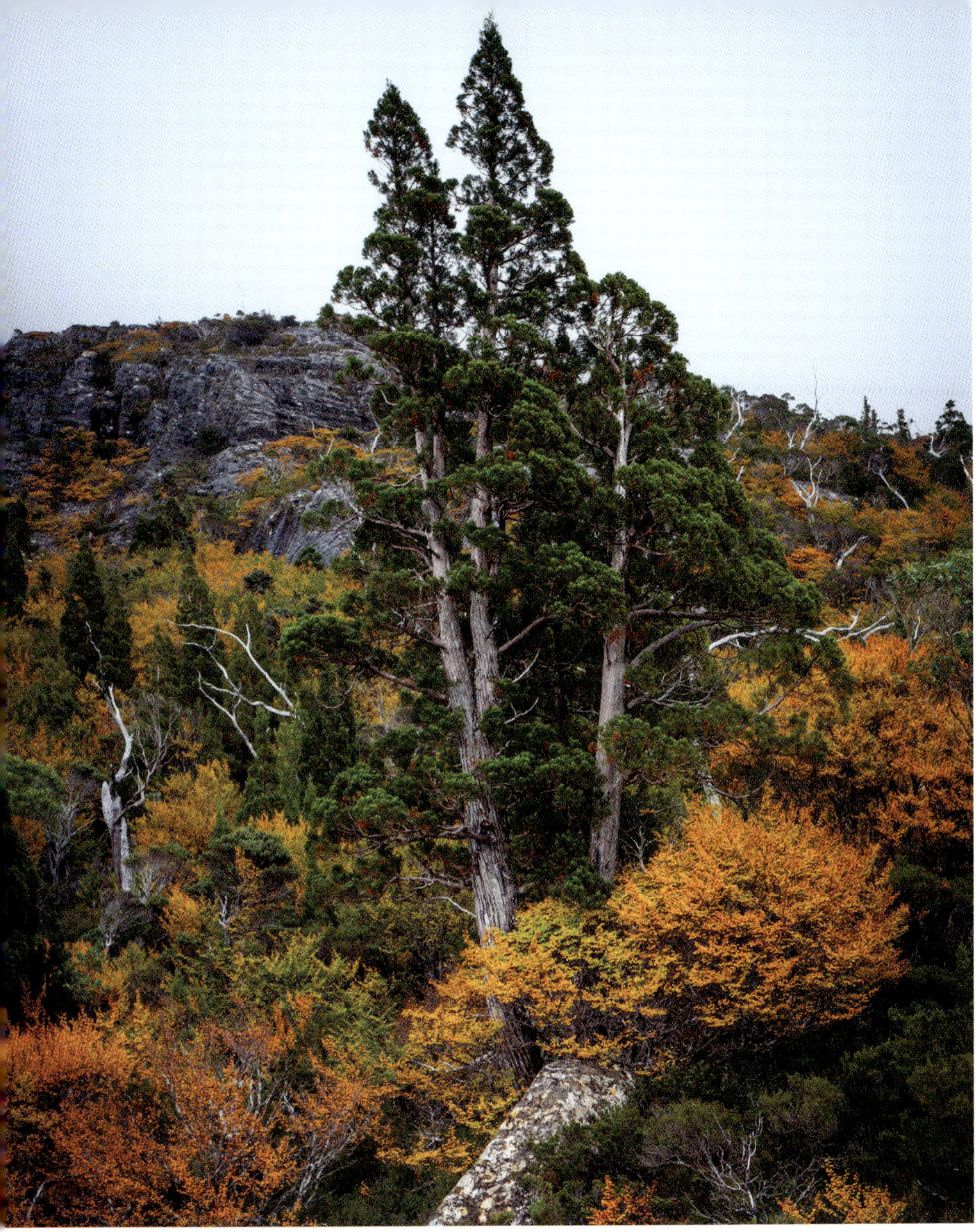

Far left: A scientist descends an 82 metre Tasmanian Swamp Gum or Mountain Ash (*Eucalyptus regnans*) in the Lower Florentine Valley near Mt Field National Park. This species is the tallest flowering plant on earth. It grows to 100 m in Tasmania thanks to heavy rainfall and infrequent fire, and lives for about 400 years.

Left and below left: Alpine and rainforest plants such as the Pencil pine, deciduous beech (*Nothofagus gunnii*) or fagus are delicate. Some species may take hundreds or even thousands of years to recover after fire and others can be badly damaged by trampling. This is why many alpine walking tracks are raised platforms and visitors are asked to stay on the path.

Middle left: Flowering melaleuca on the South Coast Track.

Below: Pandanis at Cradle Mountain. These Tasmanian plants are unrelated to the pandanus palms of the tropics.

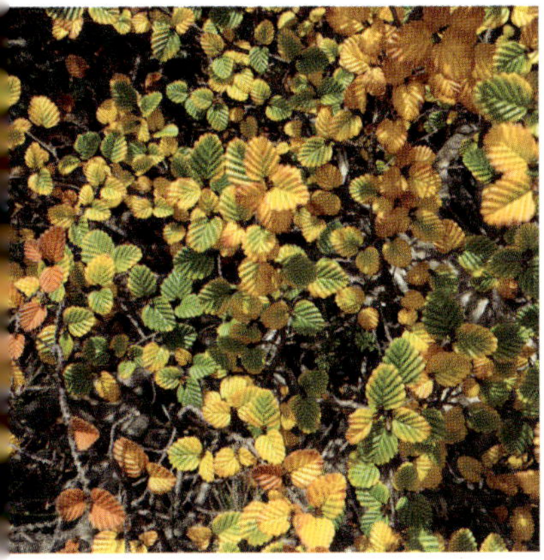

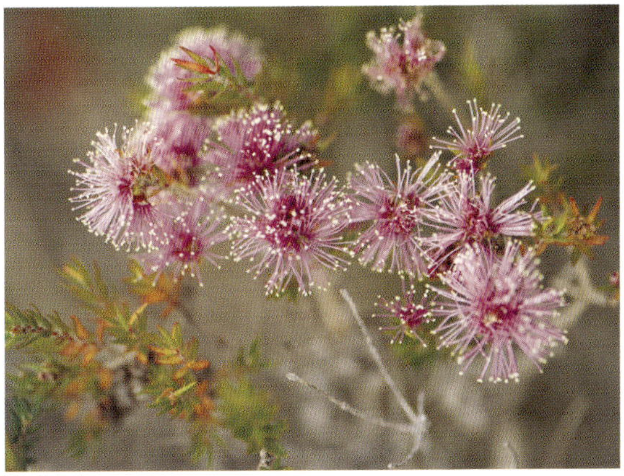

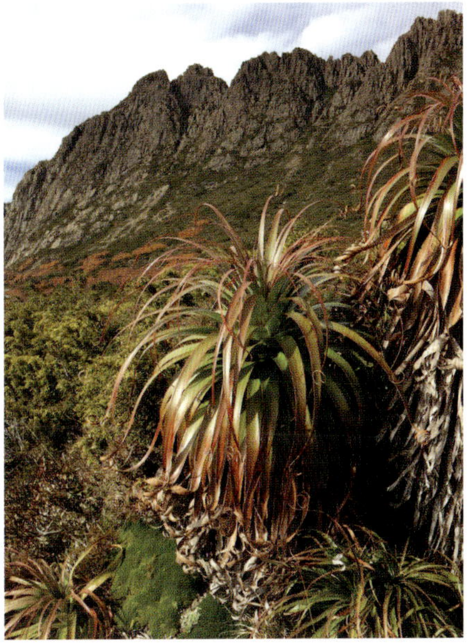

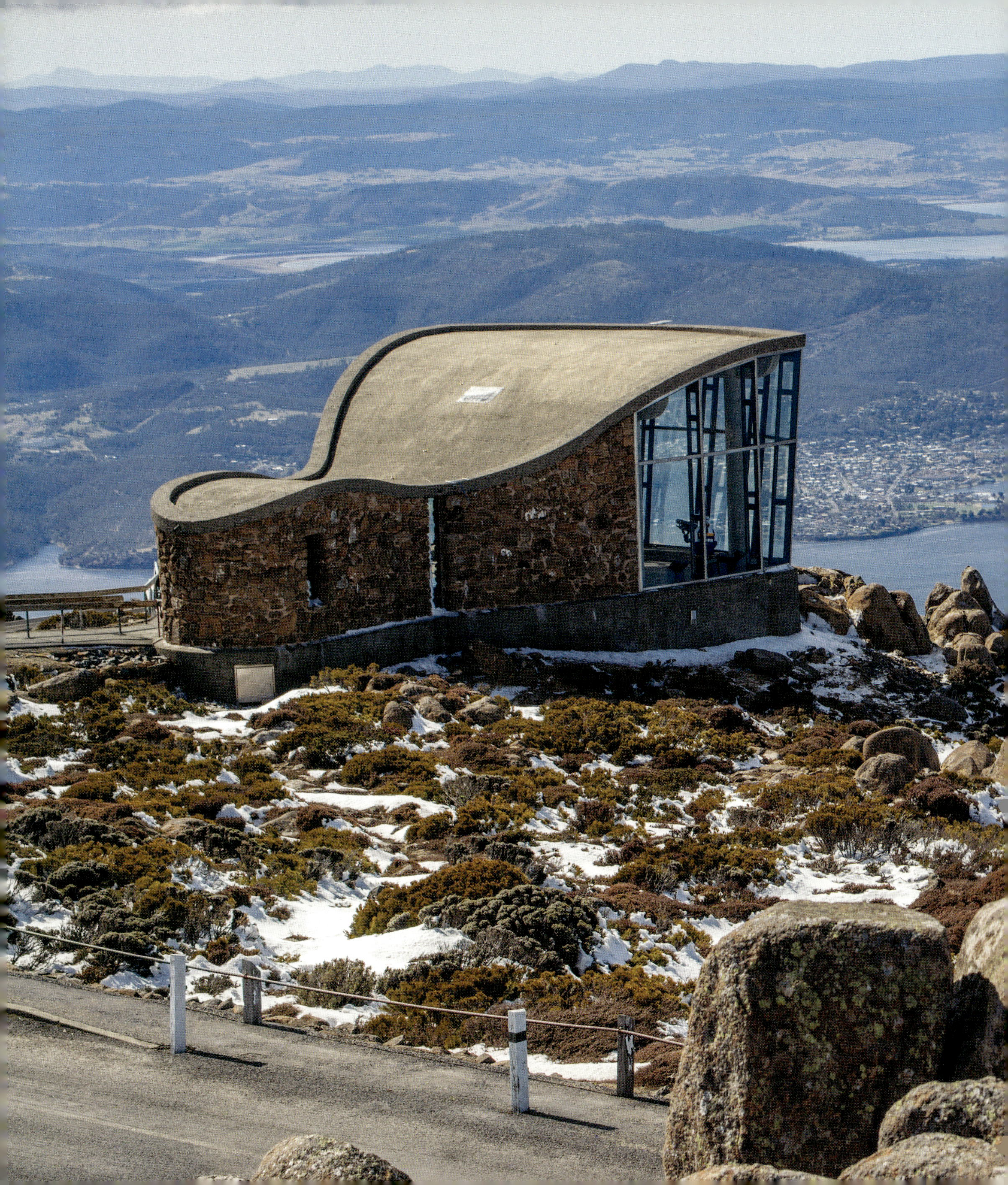

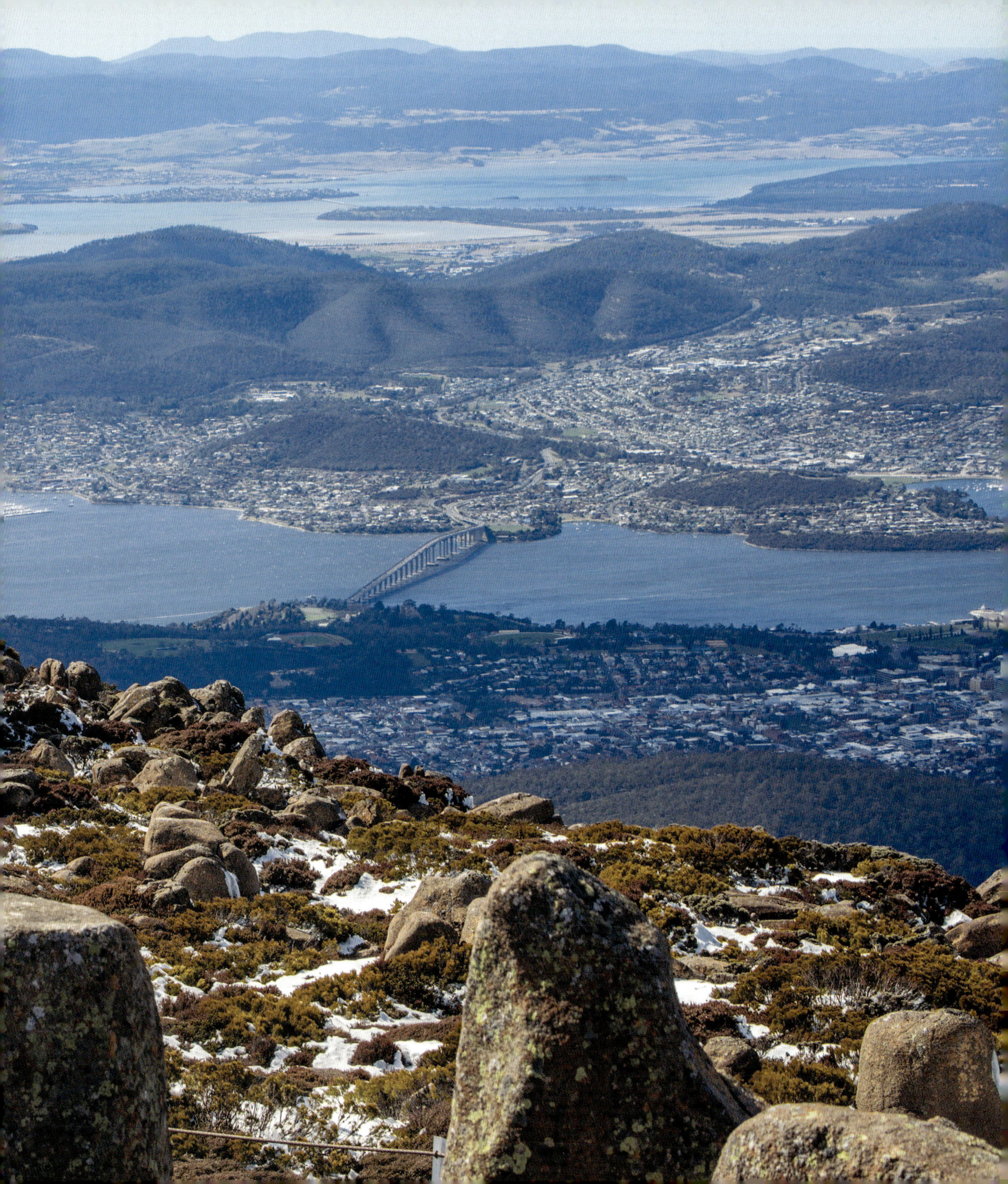

HOBART

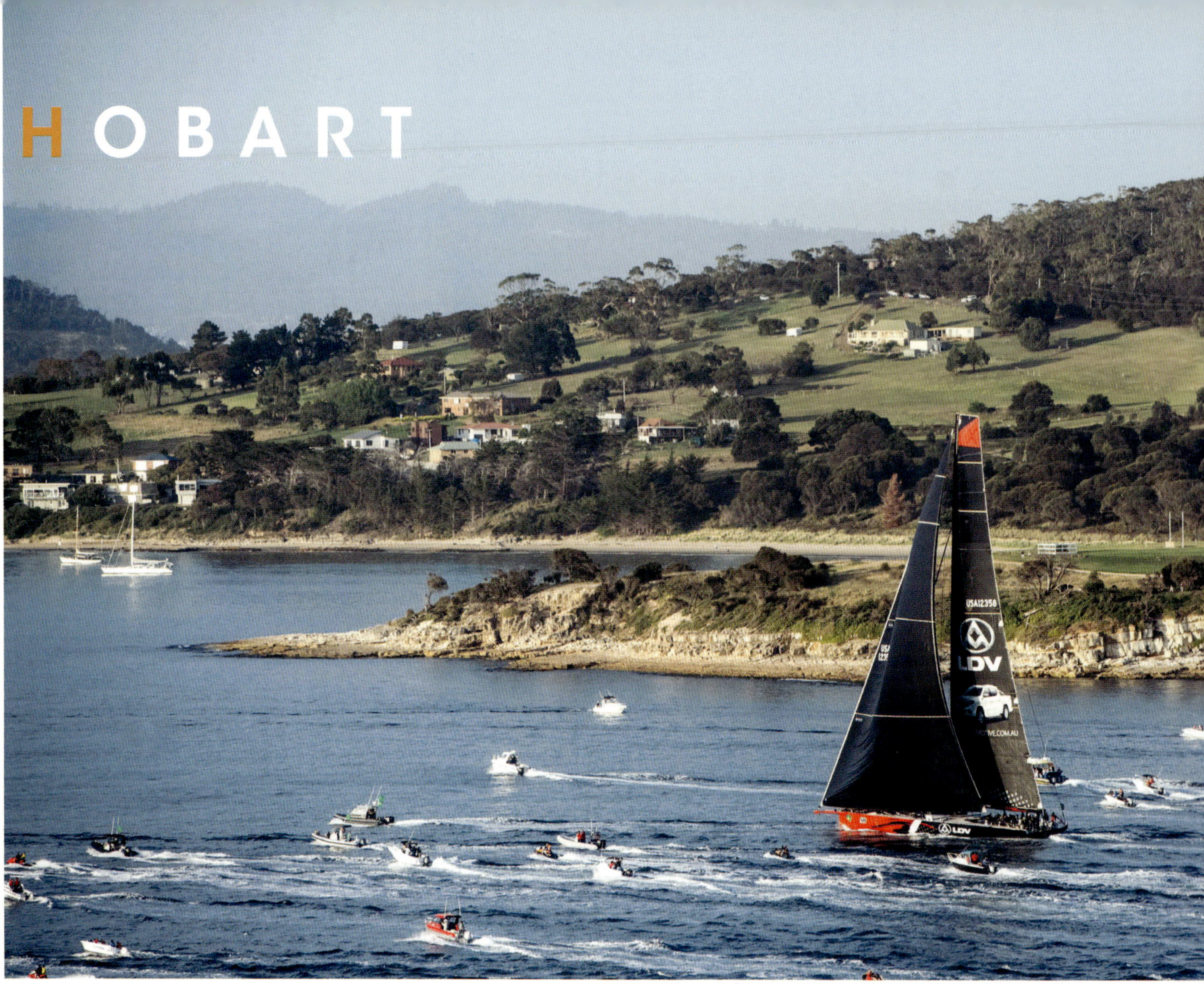

Like most harbour cities the best way to enter Hobart is by sea. The docks are lined with honey-coloured stone Georgian warehouses with the modern city rising behind, framed by the imposing bluff of Mt Wellington (1,271 m). A fine white arch spans the Derwent River and houses are scattered up the surrounding foothills. Hobart used to be a sleepy place, and with a population of just 230,000 it's still a just a fraction the size of the other state capitals, but it's the fastest growing city in Australia. Its slow pace, clean air and affordable housing makes for a very liveable city and in the last decade or so there has been an explosion of creativity, culture and gastronomy. MONA (the Museum of Old and New) is a short ferry ride upriver and one of the city's standout attractions. This gallery of contemporary and sometimes confronting art is housed in subterranean caverns and is the focus of summer and winter festivals that set the city alight. One of the best things you can do in Hobart is to eat - its flourishing food scene means you can eat at some of the best restaurants, bakeries and markets in the country. There is so much to do in Hobart that you can dip in for a few days or spend a couple of weeks exploring the city and surrounds.

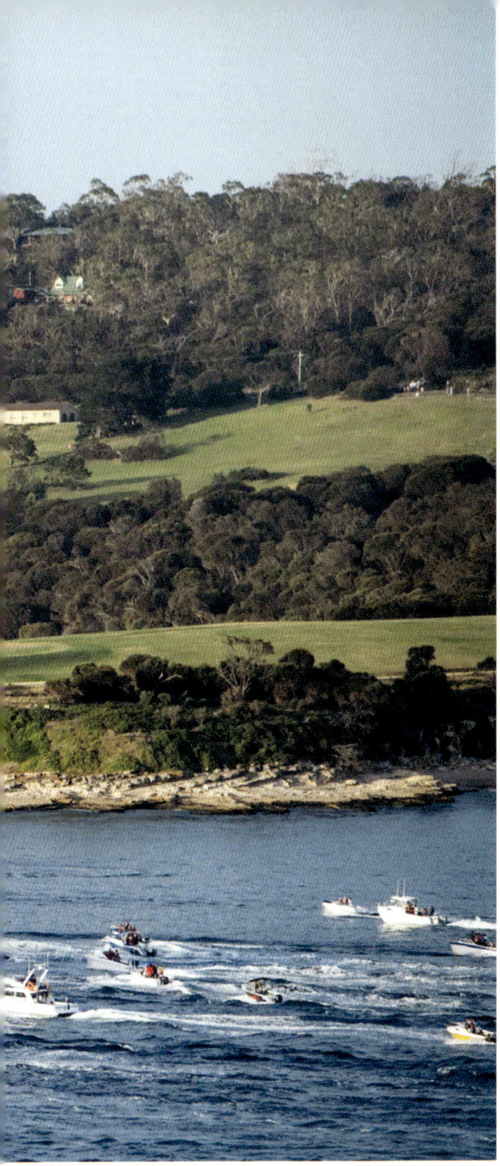

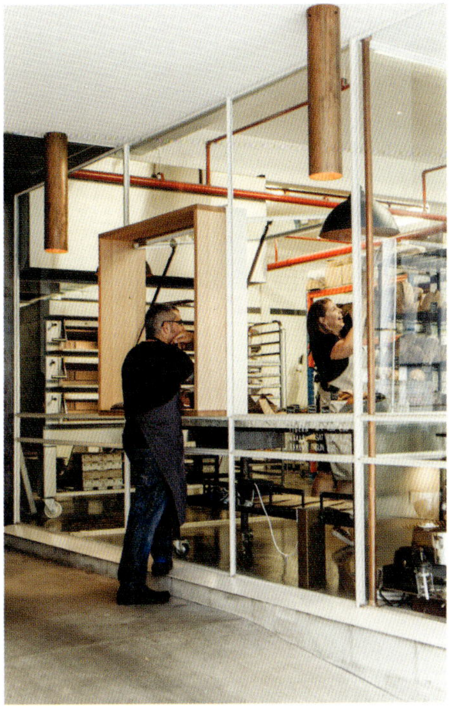

Left: Pigeon Whole Bakers, part of Hobart's exciting food scene. At weekends also try some local produce at Salamanca market on Saturdays or Farm Gate market on Sundays.

Below: Battery Point's narrow lanes and colonial-era cottages up behind Salamanca Place, are a good place for a stroll if you've over indulged.

Previous page: Hobart lies below Mt Wellington, a popular destination for challenging walking and cycling. The lookout protects visitors from very brisk summit winds.

■ The city is at its liveliest during the Sydney to Hobart Yacht Race. This legendary race starts in Sydney on Boxing Day when about 100 yachts head south for the 2-3 day journey to Hobart. It is a tough challenging race so when the yachts arrive safely at Constitution Dock the sailors and the city are ready to party.

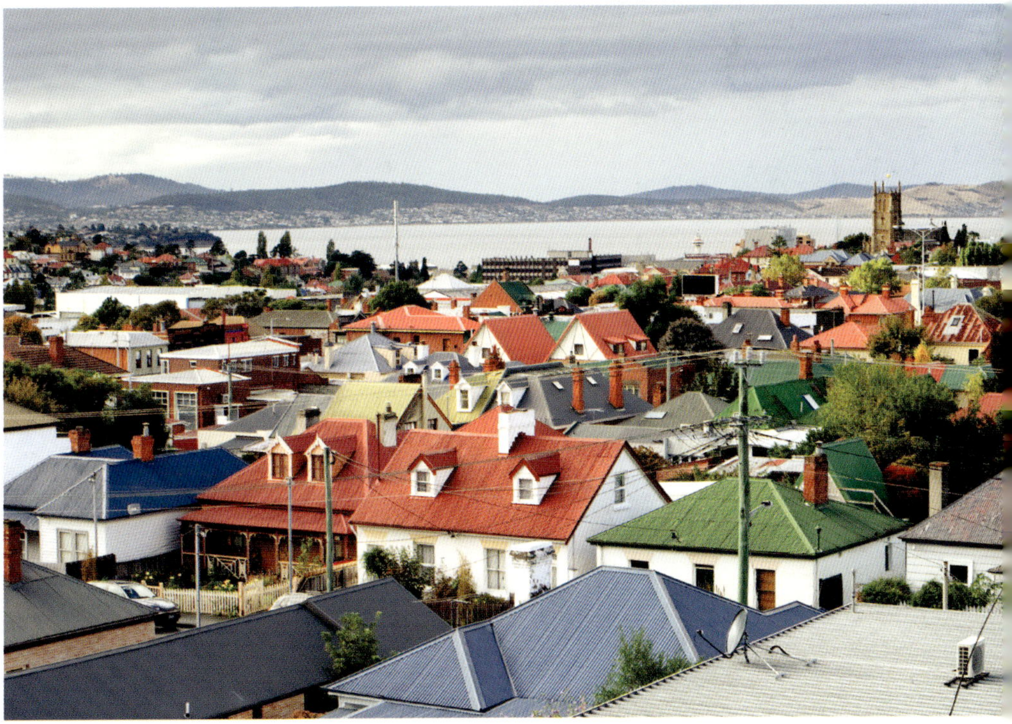

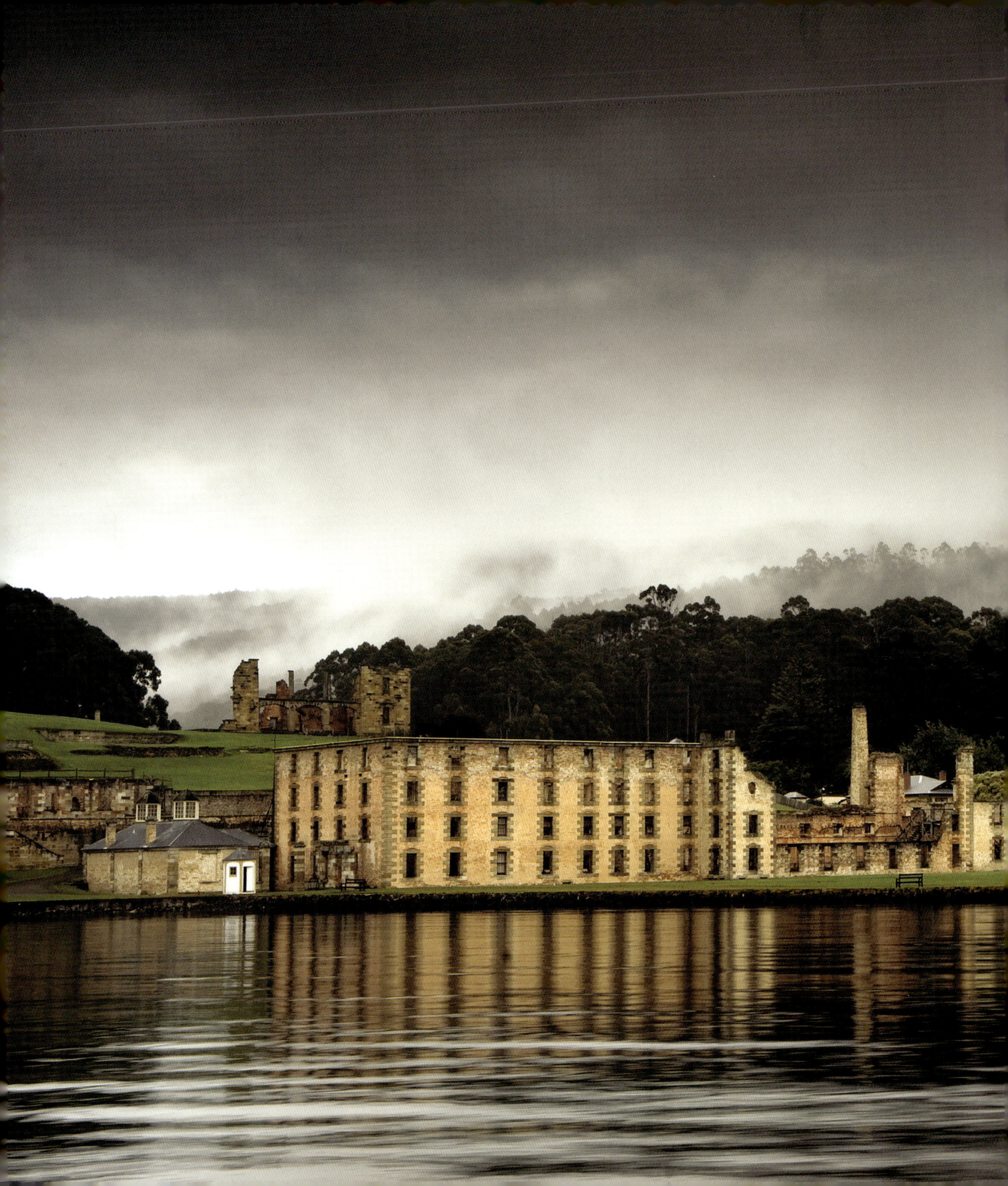

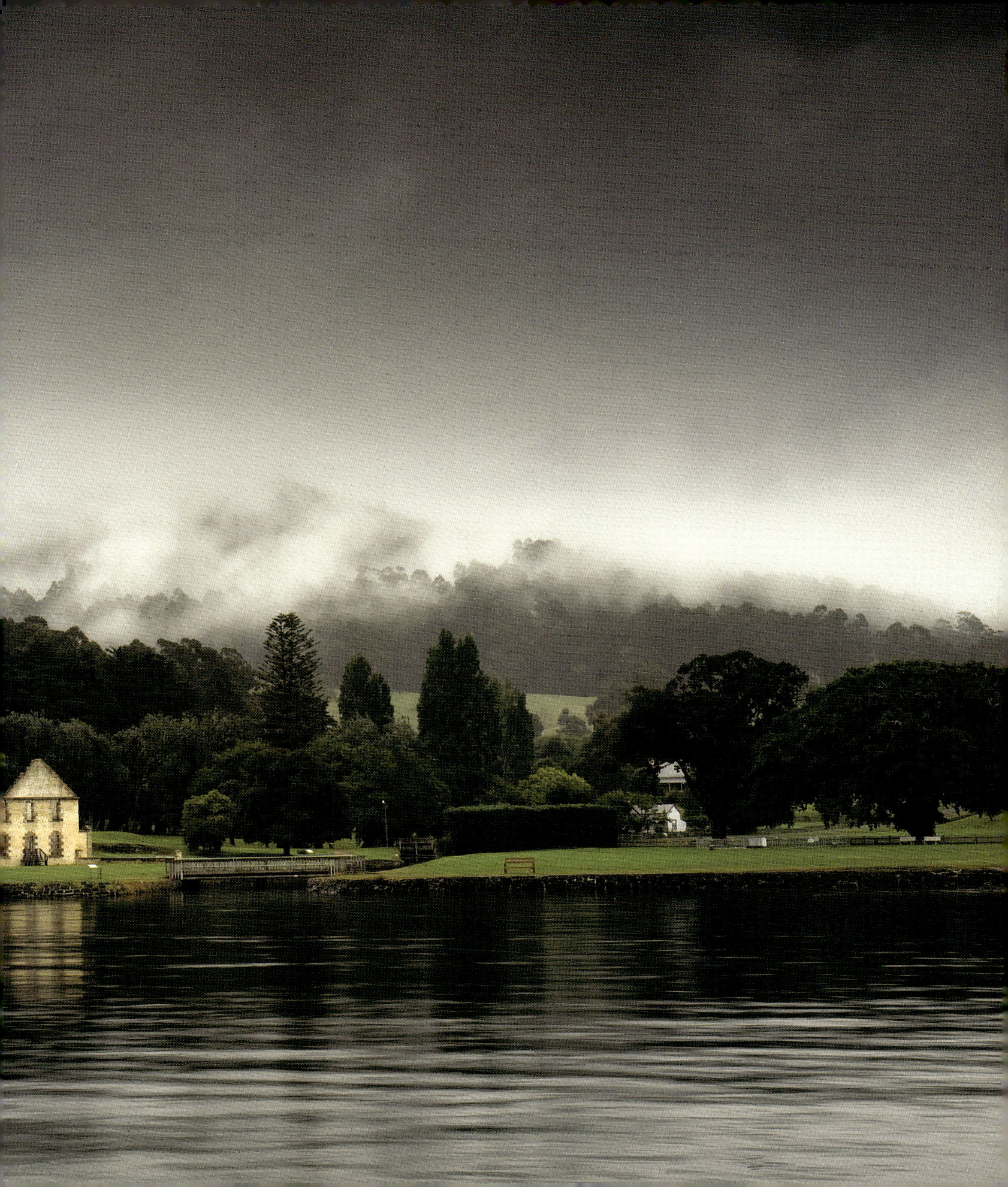

TASMAN PENINSULA

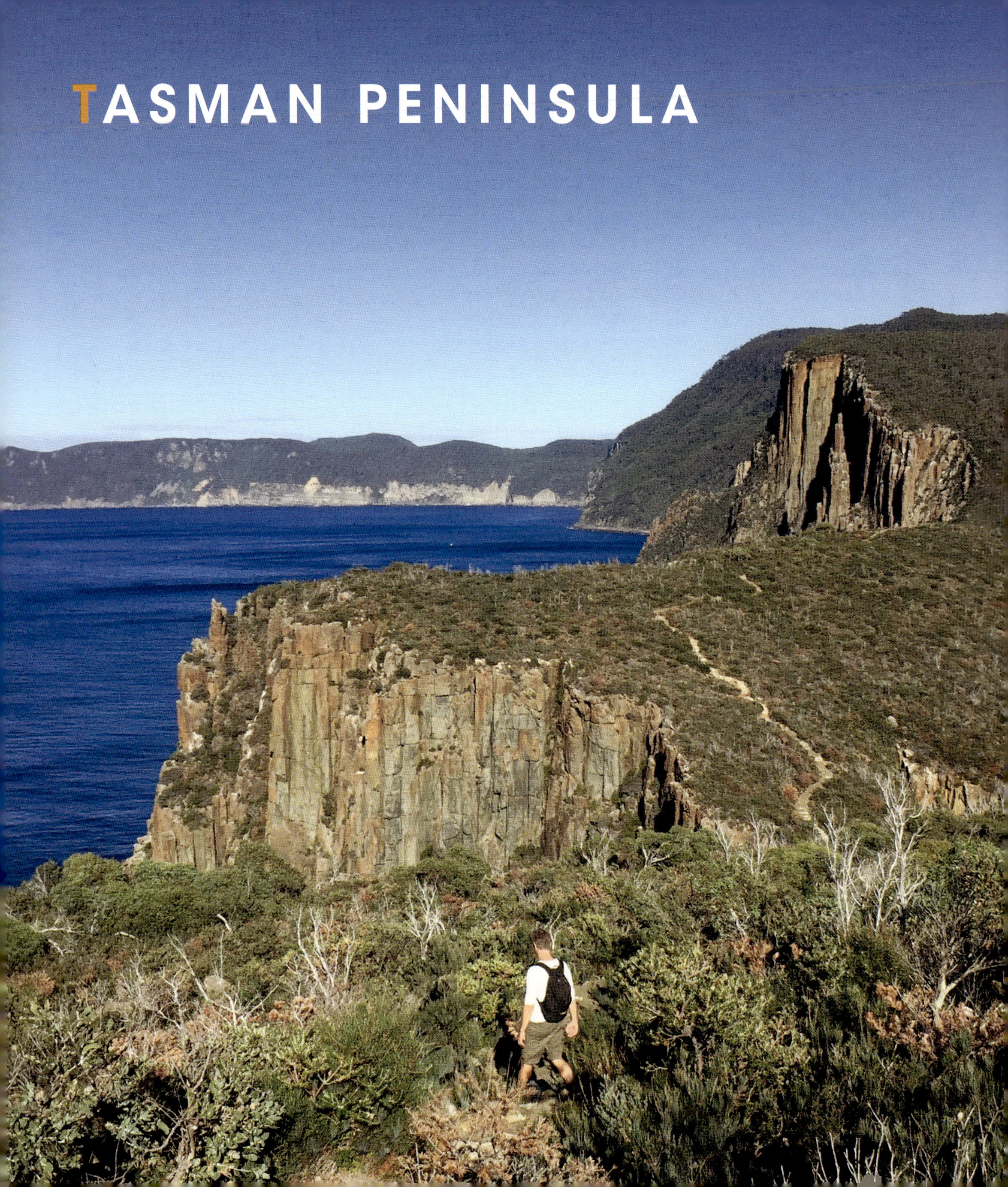

Connected to its northern neighbour the Forestier Peninsula by a pinch of sand, the Tasman was selected in 1830 to become the British Empire's principal prison-within-a-prison. Macquarie Harbour on the west coast had become unworkable and the Tasman Peninsula was not only close to Hobart but was easily sealed off from the rest of the island and had one of the best deep water ports in Van Diemen's Land. The penal settlement of Port Arthur was a place of abject misery for the 12,500 convicts who served time there until it closed in 1877. Not only was it impossible to escape from, but specialised in psychological punishment in the Separate Prison where men were kept in solitary confinement. It's a fascinating but bleak historical site and you'll need a blast of fresh salty air on the spectacular sea cliffs of the Tasman National Park, Australia's highest. The cliffs of Cape Huay, Cape Raoul and Cape Pillar are joined by the newish Three Capes Track (46 km) but you can walk shorter sections such as the vertiginous and wonderful track to Cape Huay from Fortescue Bay (4 hours return). You can also take a boat or sea kayaking tour to see the dolerite columns and cliffs up close.

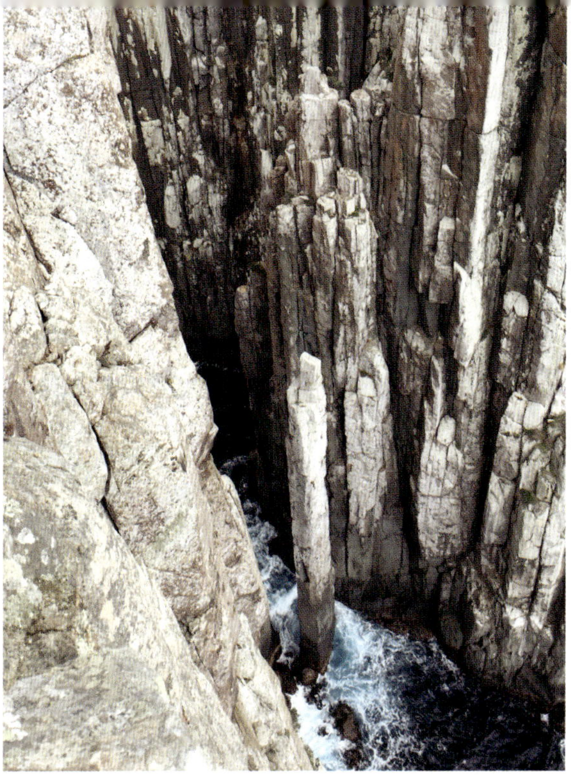

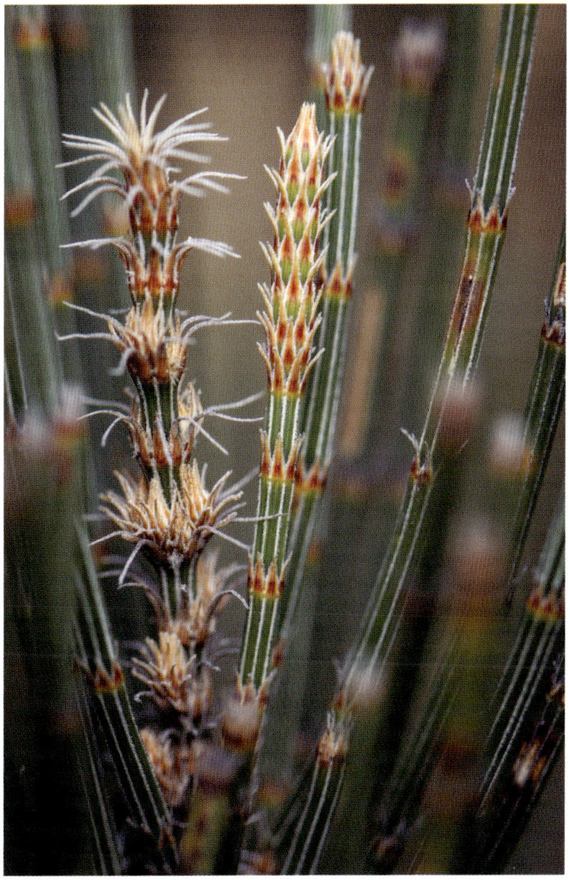

Far left: The Three Capes Track can be done as a self-guided walk (4 days) through Tasmania PWS, sleeping in comfortable self-catering cabins, or in luxury lodges with Tasmanian Walking Company.

Above: The Totem Pole, a 4 metre-wide pillar of dolerite that rises 60 m from a sea-swept notch below Cape Hauy, irresistible to rock climbers.

Left: The Tasman National Park is home to several plants found nowhere else including this Cape Pillar sheoak.

Previous page: Port Arthur's extensive historical site includes the commandant's house, hospital, guardhouse, penitentiary and model prison.

BRUNY ISLAND

This steep and narrow island, just to the south of Hobart, stretches about 75 km from tip to toe but is really two islands joined by a 5 km long sandy isthmus called the Neck. The northern half sports green rolling farmland while the rugged southern half is cloaked in forest. Accessed by car ferry from Kettering, the island has much to offer. There are beautiful walks and beaches in the south and a thriving Little Penguin colony right on the Neck, with an observation platform for visitors to view the birds as they emerge from the sea at sunset. Nearby there is a memorial to the Nuenonne people and Truganinni. There's also Cape Bruny Lighthouse to explore, surfing at Cloudy Bay, a colony of white Bennett's wallabies at Adventure Bay, plus boat cruises, and wine, cheese and oyster producers.

Right: Beach shack at Moorina Bay, Bruny Island.

Below: The tiny and endangered Forty-spotted pardalote, found only on Bruny and Maria Islands and few remote east coast habitats. Just one species of the teeming birdlife to be seen on the Labillardiere Peninsula circuit walk (6 hours) in South Bruny National Park. This walk also offers superb coastal views from coastal heathlands, beaches and forest paths.

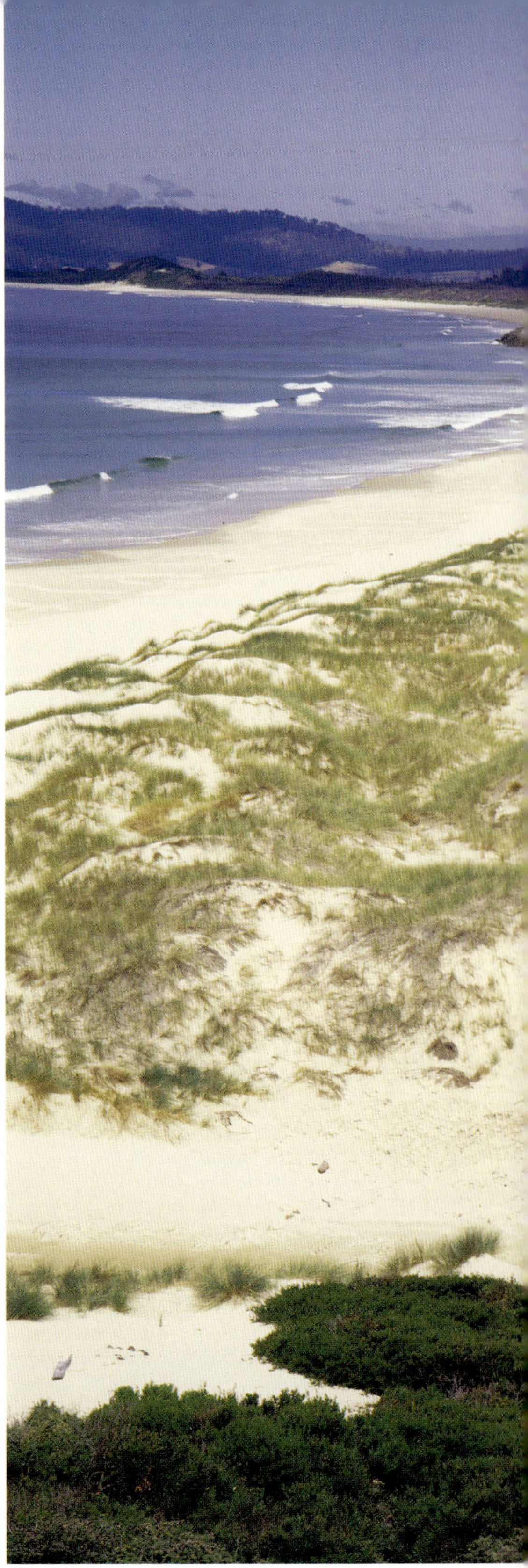

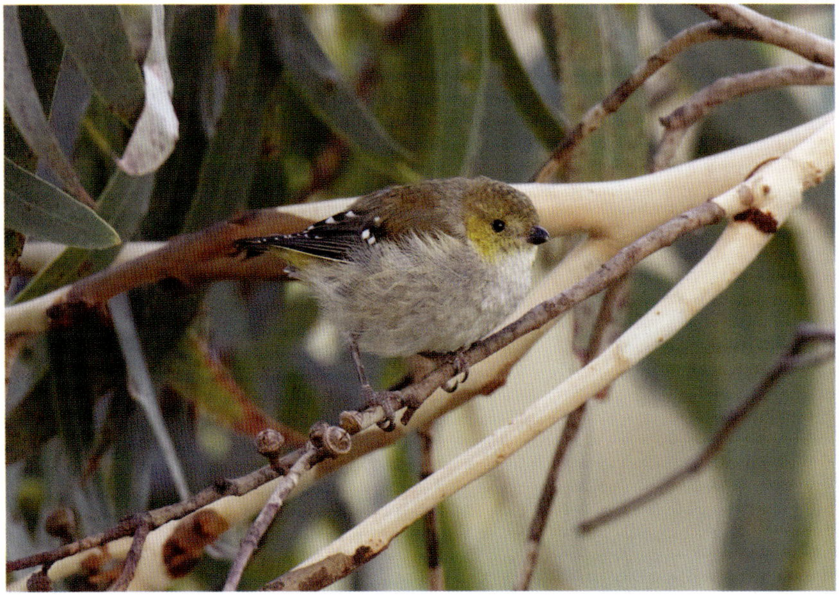

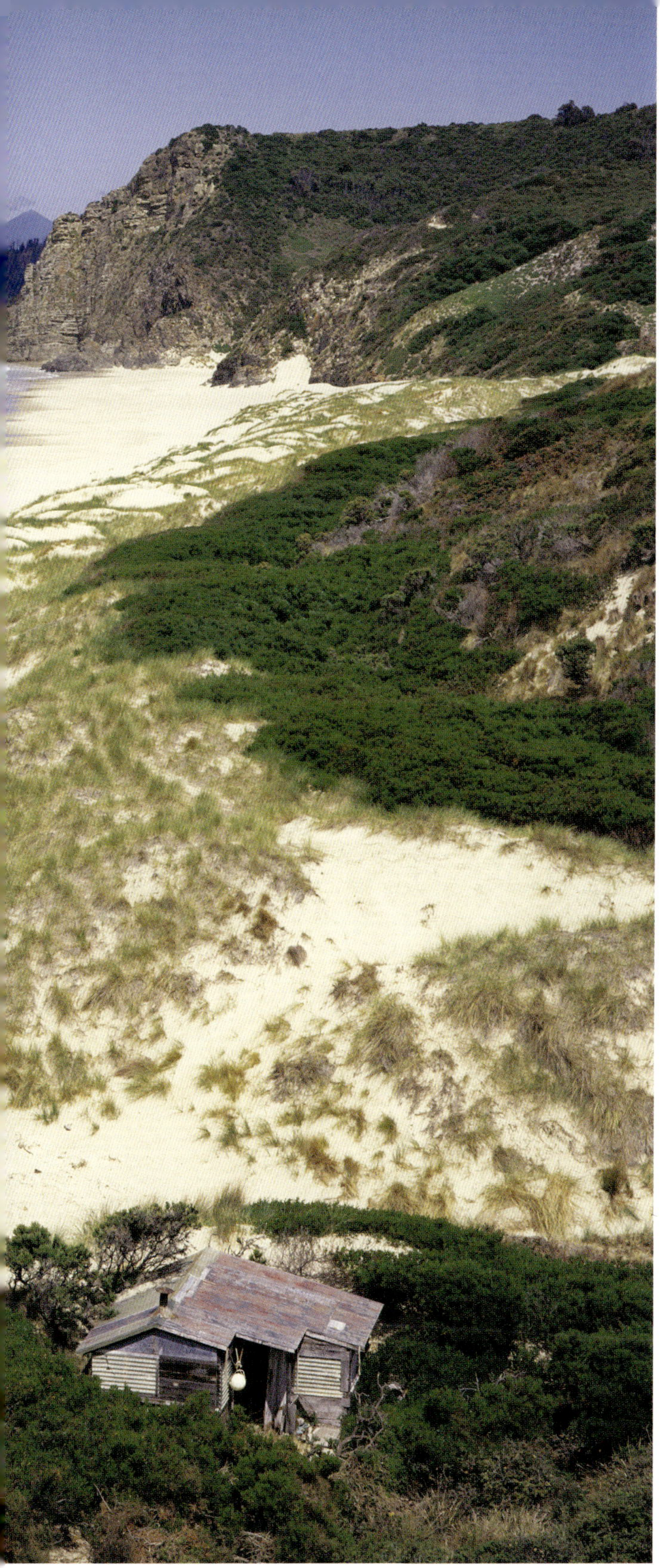

MARIA ISLAND

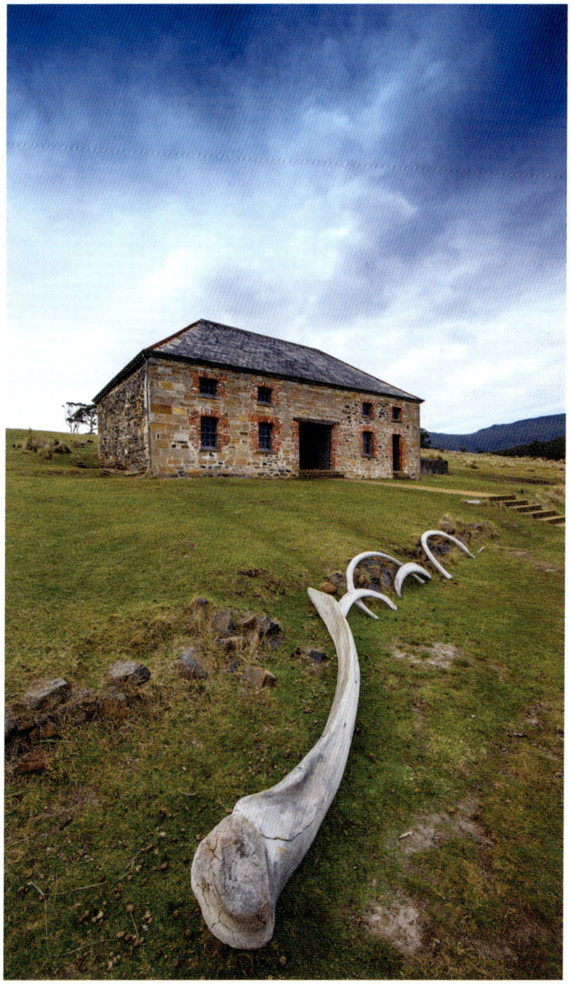

■ The Commissariat Store is a relic of Maria Island's convict past, just as the whale bones speak of its history as a whaling station in the early 1800s. The well preserved settlement at Darlington was a probation station designed to reform convicts through work, education and religious instruction. Declared a national park in 1972, Maria Island is a sanctuary for wildlife and a peaceful place for walking, mountain biking and exploring – to the Painted Cliffs or Fossil Cliffs, or climbing the summits of Bishop & Clerk (630 m) and Mt Maria (709 m) for views of the mainland. Reached by passenger ferry from Triabunna, Maria Island has campsites but no shops so you'll need to bring food or you can experience the island in comfort on the excellent 4-day guided Maria Island Walk.

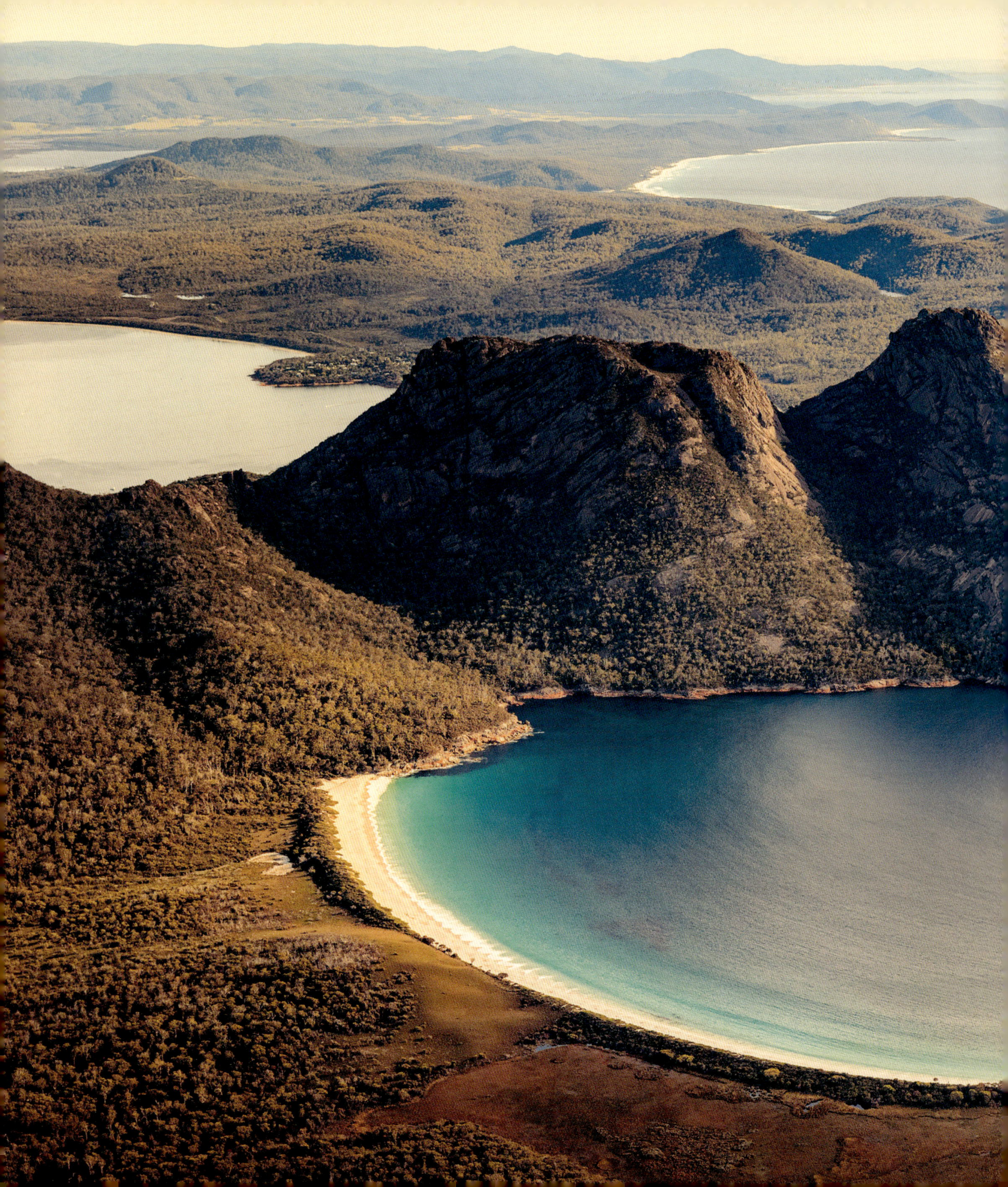

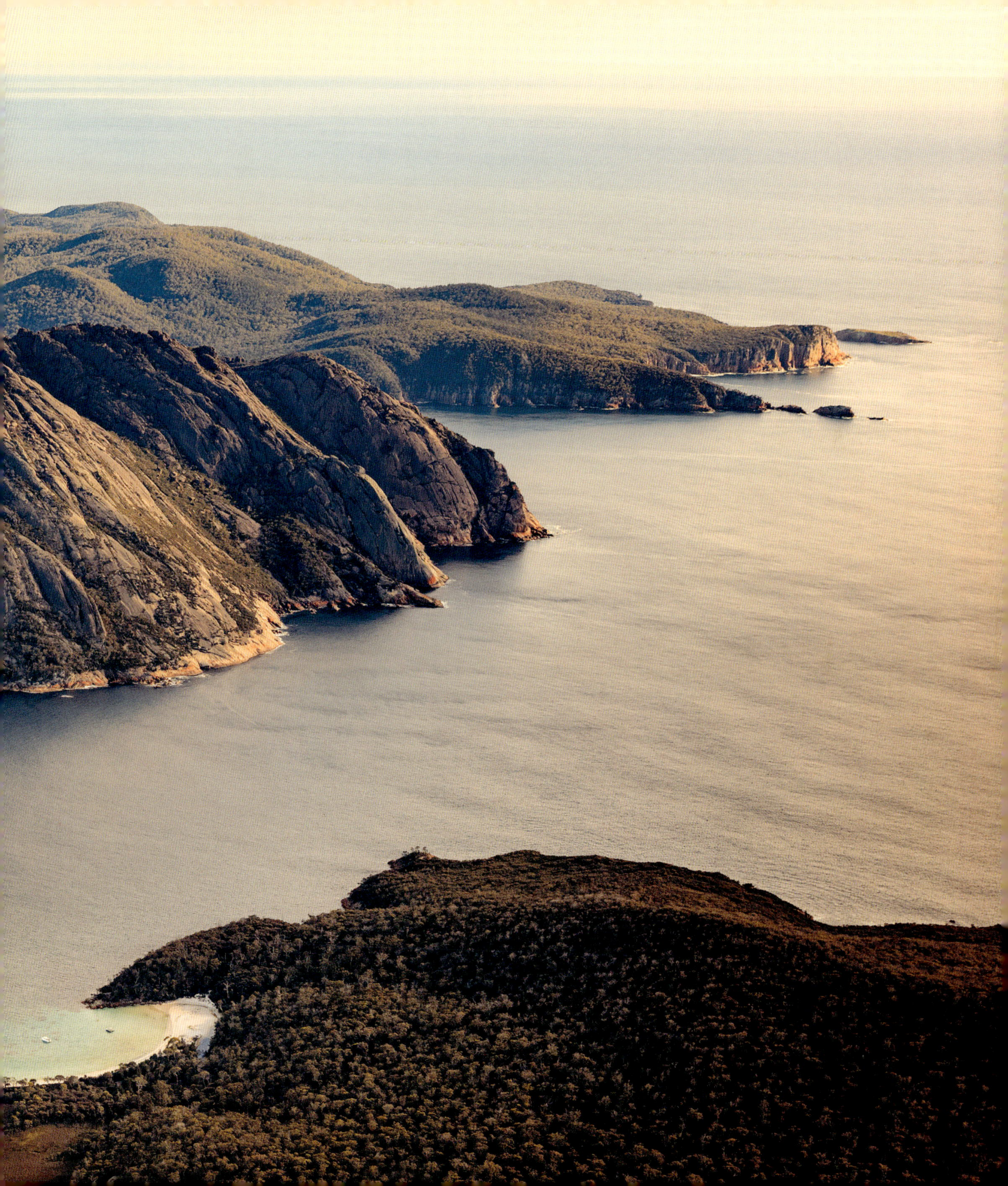

FREYCINET

Freycinet National Park, one of Australia's finest, is best known for Wineglass Bay, a perfect arc of aquamarine sea with a fine rim of white sand. Tucked behind the peachy-rose granite knuckles of the Hazards range, some effort is required to see it, which perhaps adds to the appeal. The bay is hidden from view of the eastern coast of the park and requires a half-hour steepish climb to the Wineglass Bay lookout. It's a beautiful walk but of course the park has much more to offer. There are many wonderful walking tracks, including the challenging scramble up Mt Amos and a 4-day walk along the squeaky-clean sands of the Friendly Beaches, plus good snorkeling at Sleepy Bay or more sheltered Honeymoon Bay, as well as kayaking or camping adventures. Above all, it is the colours of Freycinet that beguile – the pink stone, the glassy blue water, orange lichen and green cloak of eucalypt forest. Don't miss a stroll at sunset when the park glows in the warm light, wine tasting at nearby vineyards or try some freshly shucked local oysters.

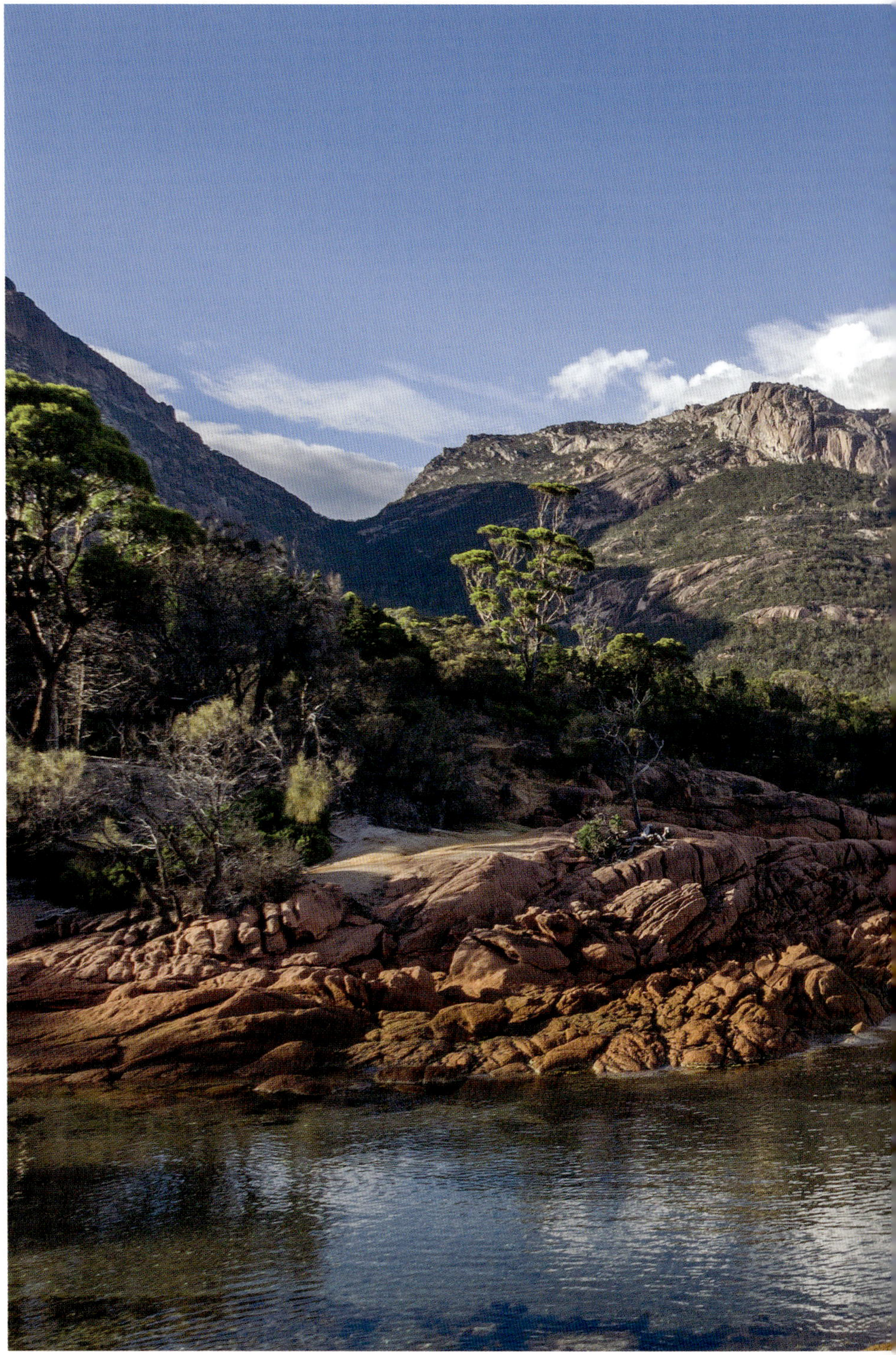

■ Right: The pink granite of the Hazards range comes from iron oxide impurities in feldspar, one of the common minerals found in granite. The others are black mica and white quartz.

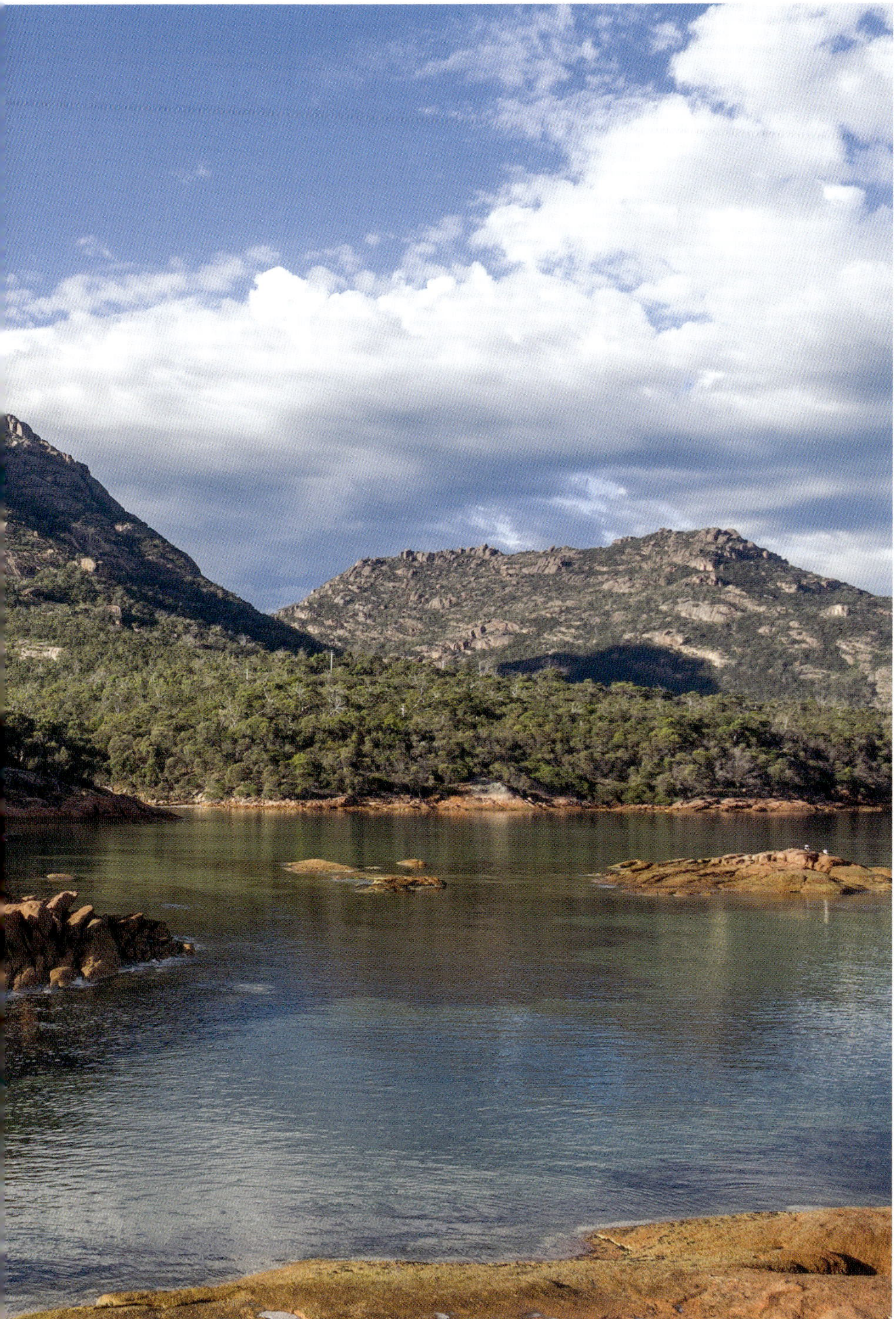

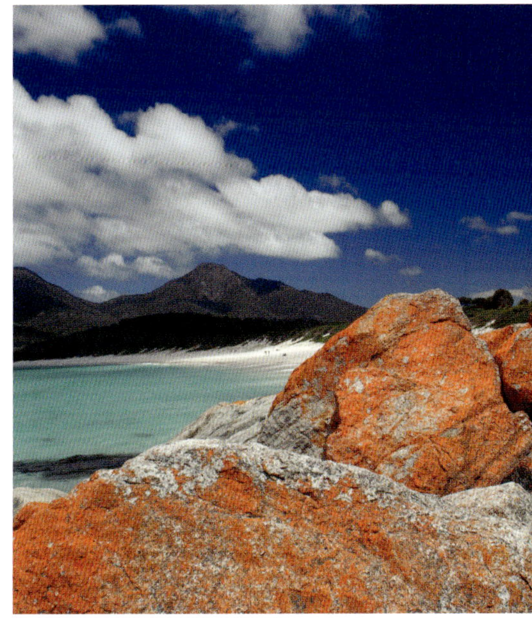

Above: Unlike the dolerite rock of other parts of the state, the east coast is dominated by granite, which breaks down into the cleanest and whitest beaches imaginable. The east coast of Tasmania harbours some superb examples, at Wineglass Bay, the Bay of Fires and Mount William National Park. The clean sand contributes to sparkling transparent water, providing superb swimming, snorkeling, and diving conditions.

Previous page: Wineglass Bay and the Hazards range, looking towards the northern end of the park. It's 45 minutes from the Wineglass Bay lookout down to the beach from where you can retrace your steps or continue across the isthmus and back around the coastline to Coles Bay (4-5 hours, 11 km circuit).

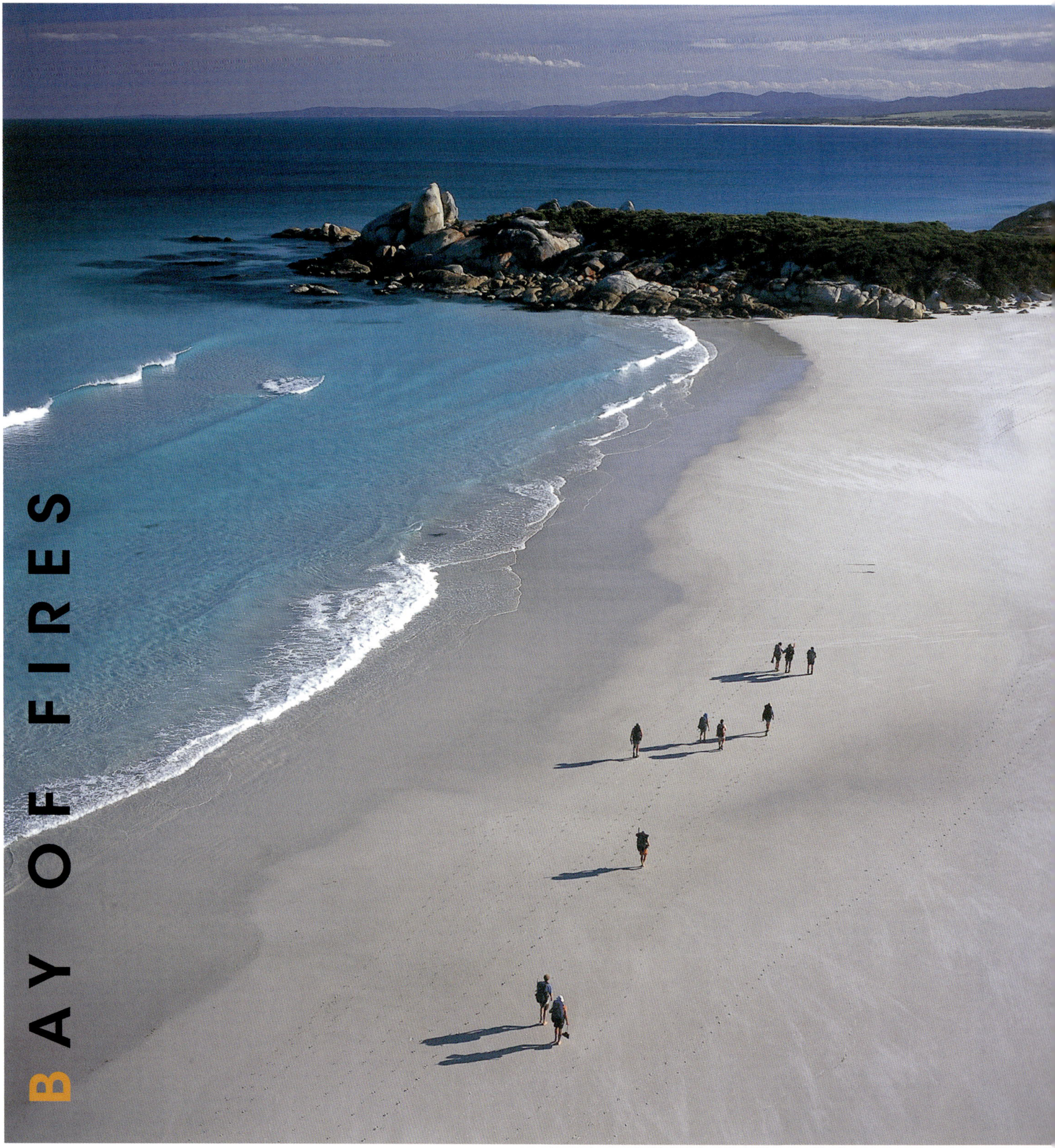
BAY OF FIRES

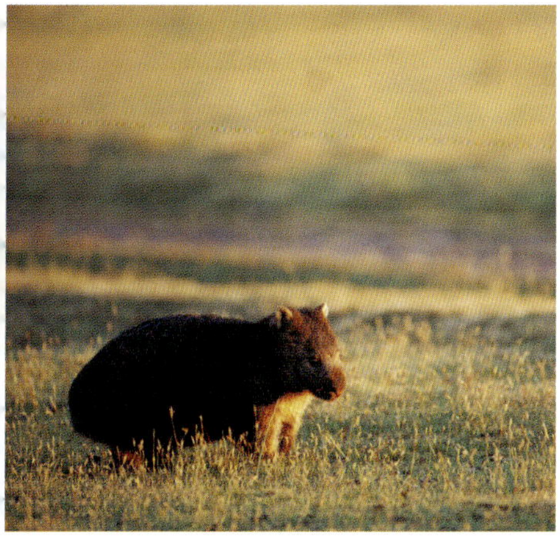

The north-easterly tip of Tasmania is encompassed by the remote Mt William National Park and the Bay of Fires, a long expanse of perfect sand, as fine and white as sugar. Established in 1971 as a sanctuary for Tasmania's only Kangaroo species, the Forester (Eastern Grey), the park remains a magical place to see wildlife roaming over the 'marsupial lawn' at dawn and dusk. Kangaroos, pademelons, wallabies, wombats, and echidnas browse along Forester Kangaroo Drive, in the northern end of the park, where there are campsites in the dunes at Stumpy's Bay. At night you might even hear the screeches and growls of quolls and devils. By day you can walk up diminutive Mt William (216 m) or walk the endless white beaches, clamber over granite boulders splashed with distinctive orange lichen and swim in the crystal clear sea. There is much to learn on the Aboriginal-owned 4-day Wukalina walk if time allows or walk from Stumpy's Bay to Deep Creek campground (15 km, 6-7 hours). The Bay of Fires at the southern end of the park was named by Captain Tobias Furneaux who saw fires on shore as he sailed by in 1773, and stretches 50 km from Eddystone Point in the north to Binalong Bay in the south.

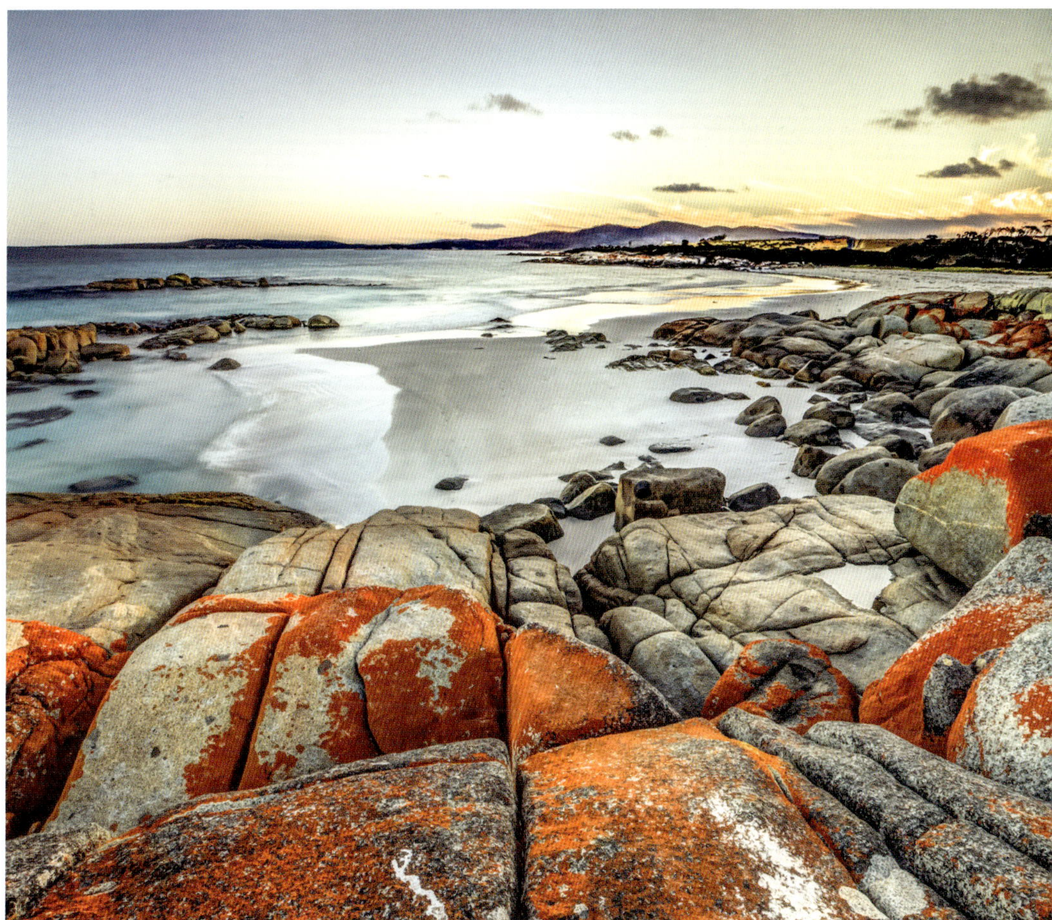

Above: Wombat grazing at sunset in Mt William National Park.

Left: Walking the Bay of Fires. To explore this coastline there are campsites and accommodation around Binalong Bay but if you like a long and luxurious walk, the 4-day Bay of Fires walk includes two nights at the Bay of Fires eco-lodge.

Right: The orange colour on these rocks is a lichen belonging to the family *Hymeneliaceae*, which thrives on east coast shorelines.

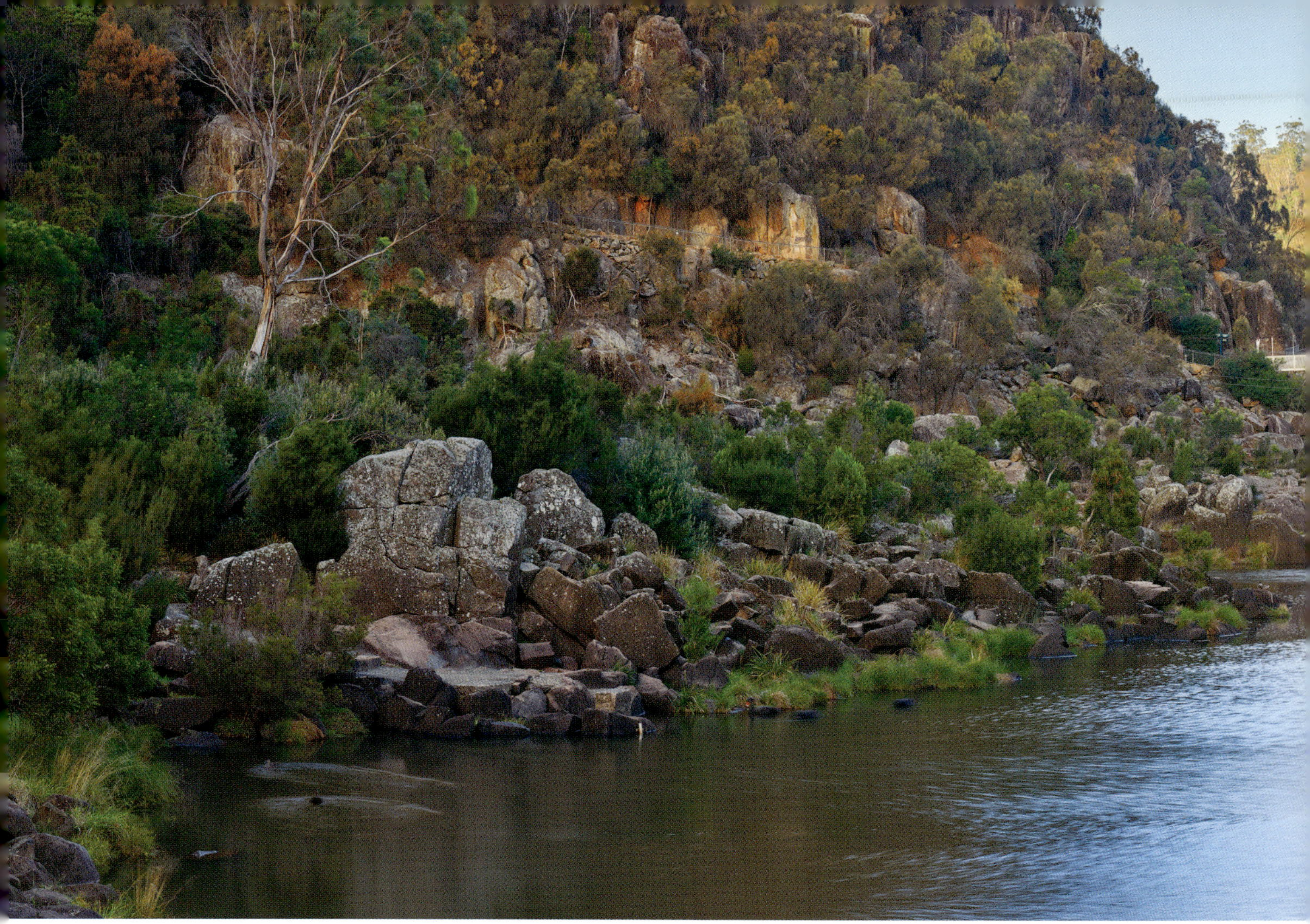

LAUNCESTON & BEN LOMOND

Tasmania's second largest city is a gracious river city and makes a useful base for visitors to the northern part of the state. Surrounded by hills at the head of the Tamar Valley, Launceston was established in 1806 and contains some of the country's finest examples of Colonial and Victorian architecture. It's well worth a stroll around the beautiful streets, parks and gardens of this compact city but its jewel is lovely Cataract Gorge with a wealth of bushwalks plus a swimming pool, chairlift, tea rooms and Victorian fern garden. Head north of the city to explore the fertile Tamar Valley's wetlands, vineyards and orchards, and right at the tip is Narawntapu National Park, where wombats and wallabies can be found grazing on the lawn at dusk. To the south, you'll find the huge massif of Ben Lomond, visible from nearly 100 km away. From the summit at Legges Tor (1,572 m) much of the island state can be seen on a clear day. The flat-topped mountain, with its battlements of dark, brooding pillars, is pure Gothic fantasy. The unsealed access road ascends a route so steep, twisting and exposed it is known as Jacob's Ladder.

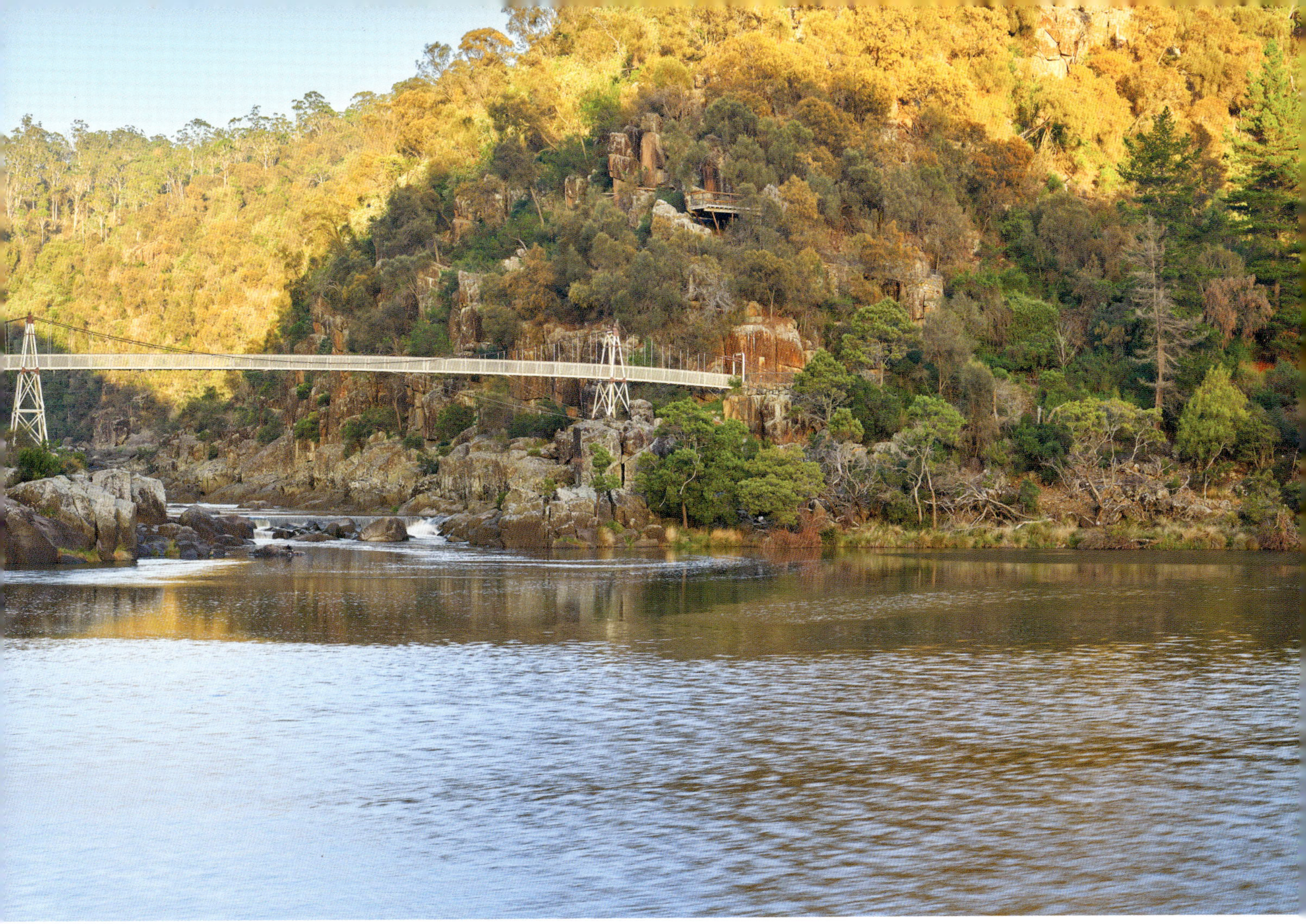

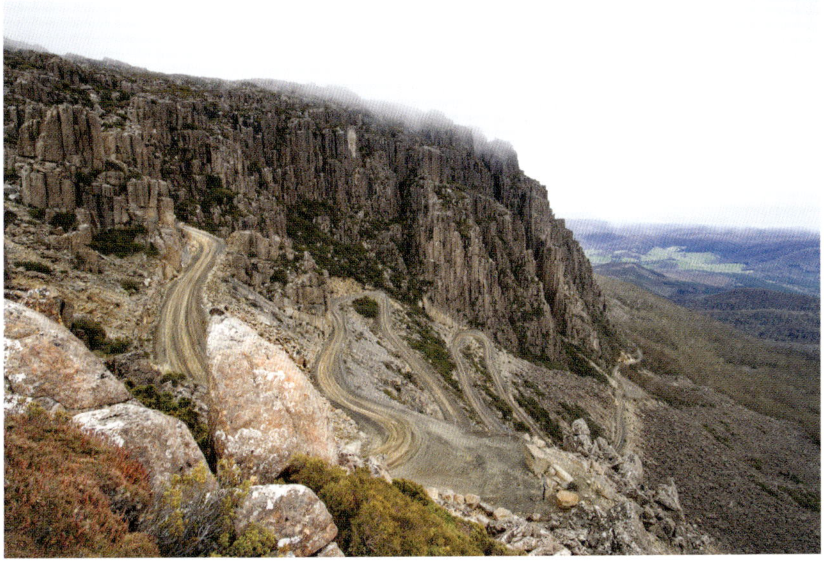

Above: The Alexandra Suspension Bridge in Cataract Gorge is the highlight of a wonderful circuit walk. Starting at mouth of the gorge at Kings Bridge, take the steep Zig Zag track up to the bridge or chairlift, then return via the flat and easy Cataract Walk (3 hour circuit).

Left: Ben Lomond is the state's main skifield and the season runs from July to September. In summer you can walk up the plateau to the summit (about 2 hours one way) for wonderful views but as this is alpine country you need to be prepared for all conditions. Of course, Jacob's Ladder, one of Tasmania's most spectacular short drives, must first be negotiated with great care!

GREAT WESTERN TIERS

Driving west from Launceston, towards Cradle Mountain, you pass through rich pastoral river valleys rising to the impressive dark citadels of the Great Western Tiers, marking the edge of Tasmania's magnificent alpine country, the Central Plateau. Quamby Bluff (1226 m) dominates the area, just south of Deloraine. This charming small town makes an ideal base to explore the many attractions of this region. Walkers have countless options, from a short walk to dramatic Devil's Gullett lookout (20 mins return), Meander Falls (10 km), climbing Quamby Bluff or Mt Roland (1234 m, both 5 hours return) or a walk through myrtle rainforest to very lovely Liffey Falls (45 mins). Around Mole Creek, a little further west, there are about 300 caves in the karst (limestone) landscape protected by the Mole Creek Karst National Park. The Marakoopa and King Solomons Caves can be explored on guided tours. Mole Creek is also home to Trowunna, one of Tasmania's best wildlife parks, especially if you are interested in Tasmanian devils as these nocturnal scavengers are not easy to see in the wild.

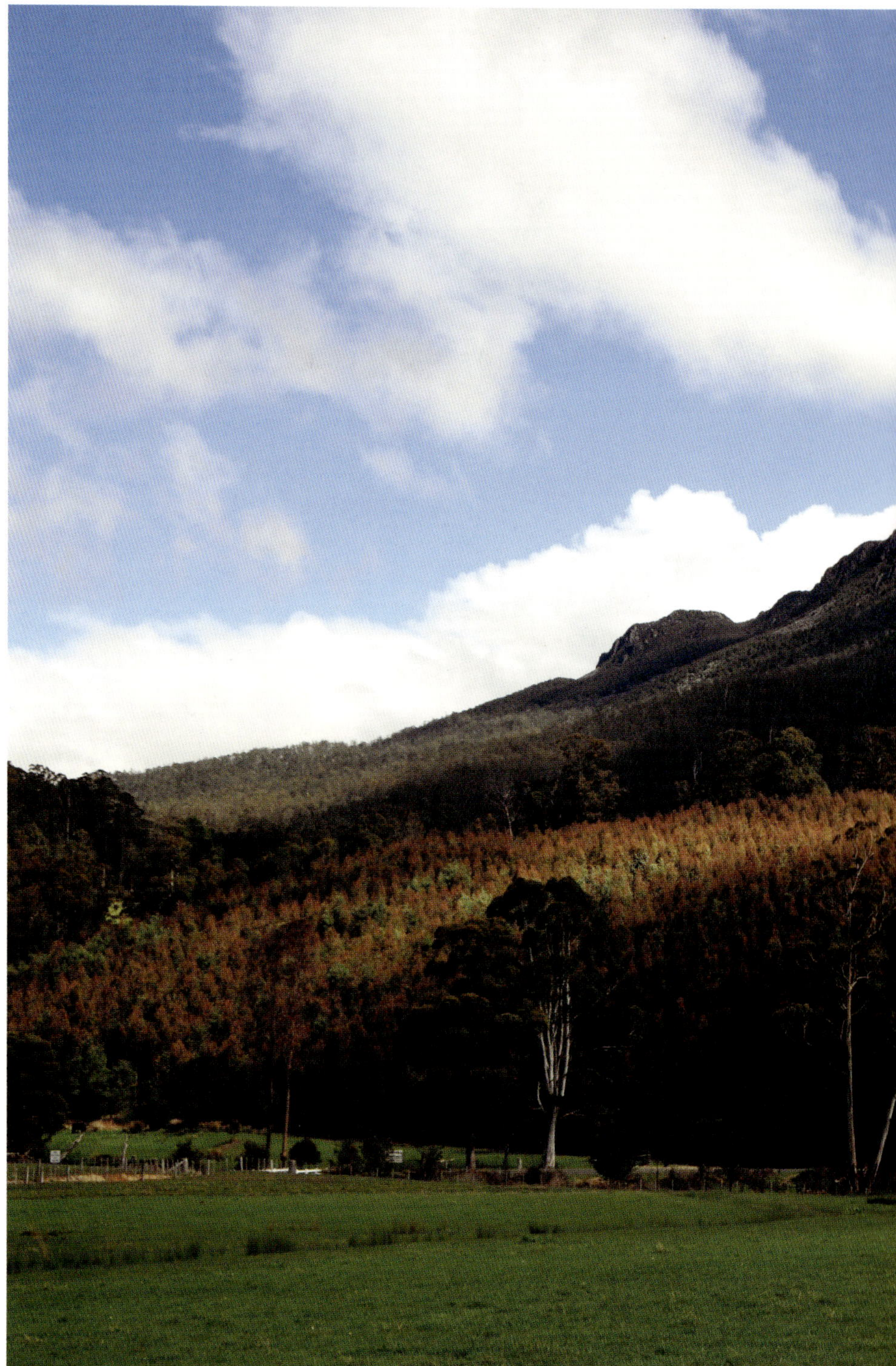

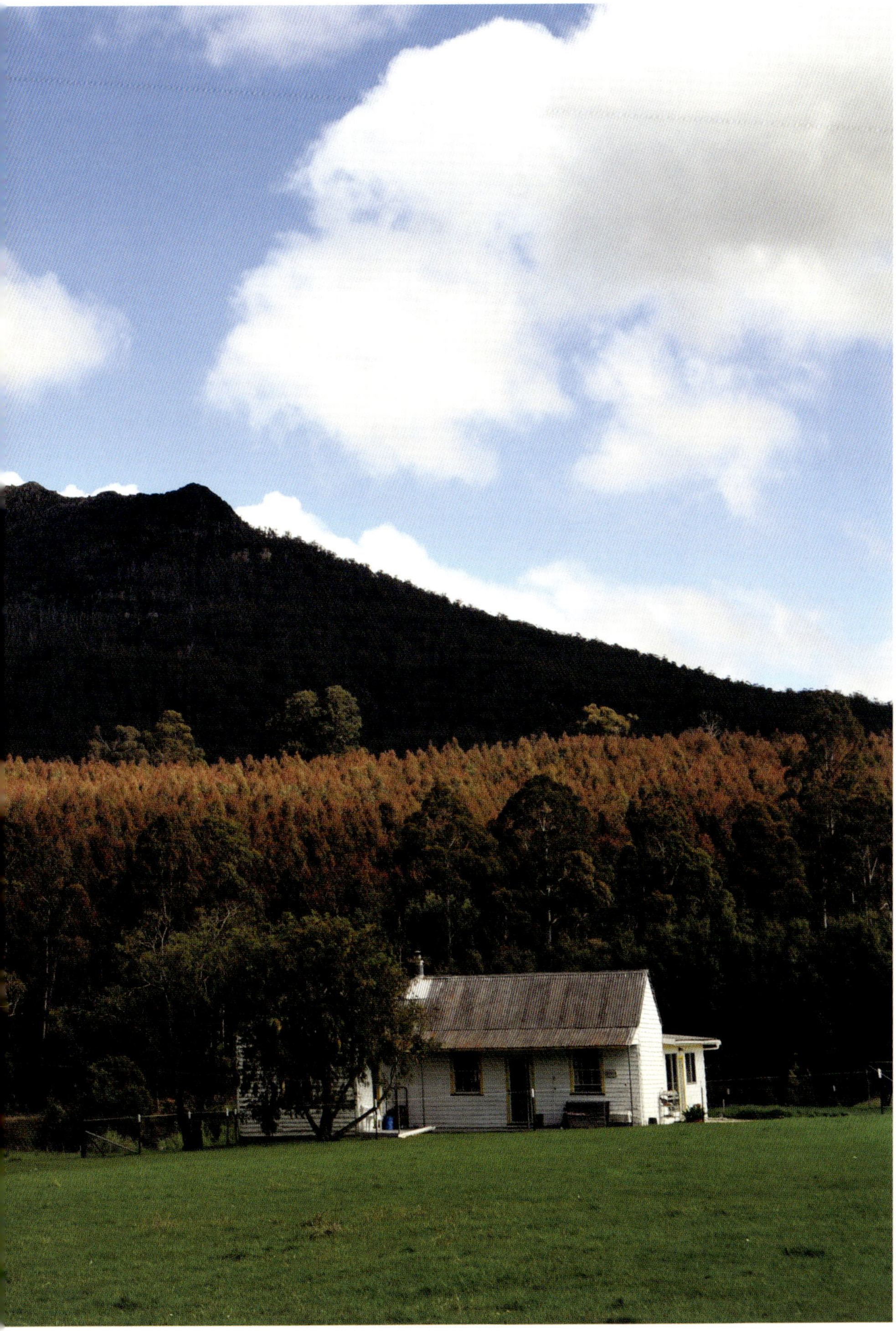

Left: Quamby Bluff above Golden Valley. The walk from Highland Lakes Road to the top is very steep with a lot of scrambling over boulders near the summit but the reward is that most of northern Tasmania can be seen from the top (7 km).

Below: Tasmanian devil at Trowunna Wildlife Sanctuary. Trowunna's devil conservation breeding program has been running for more than 30 years and has bred 16 generations of devils. Tours and devil feeding three times daily.

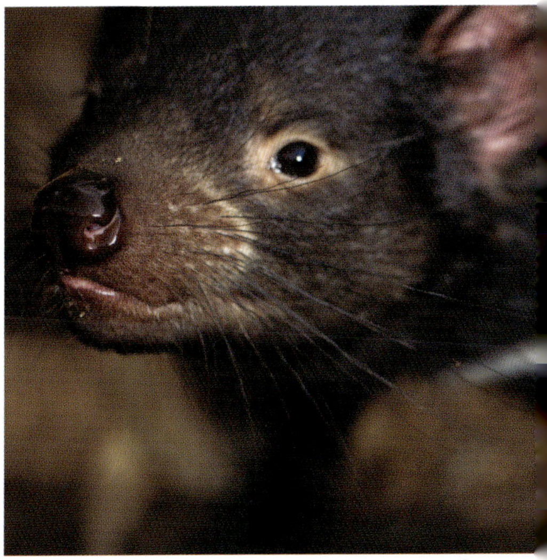

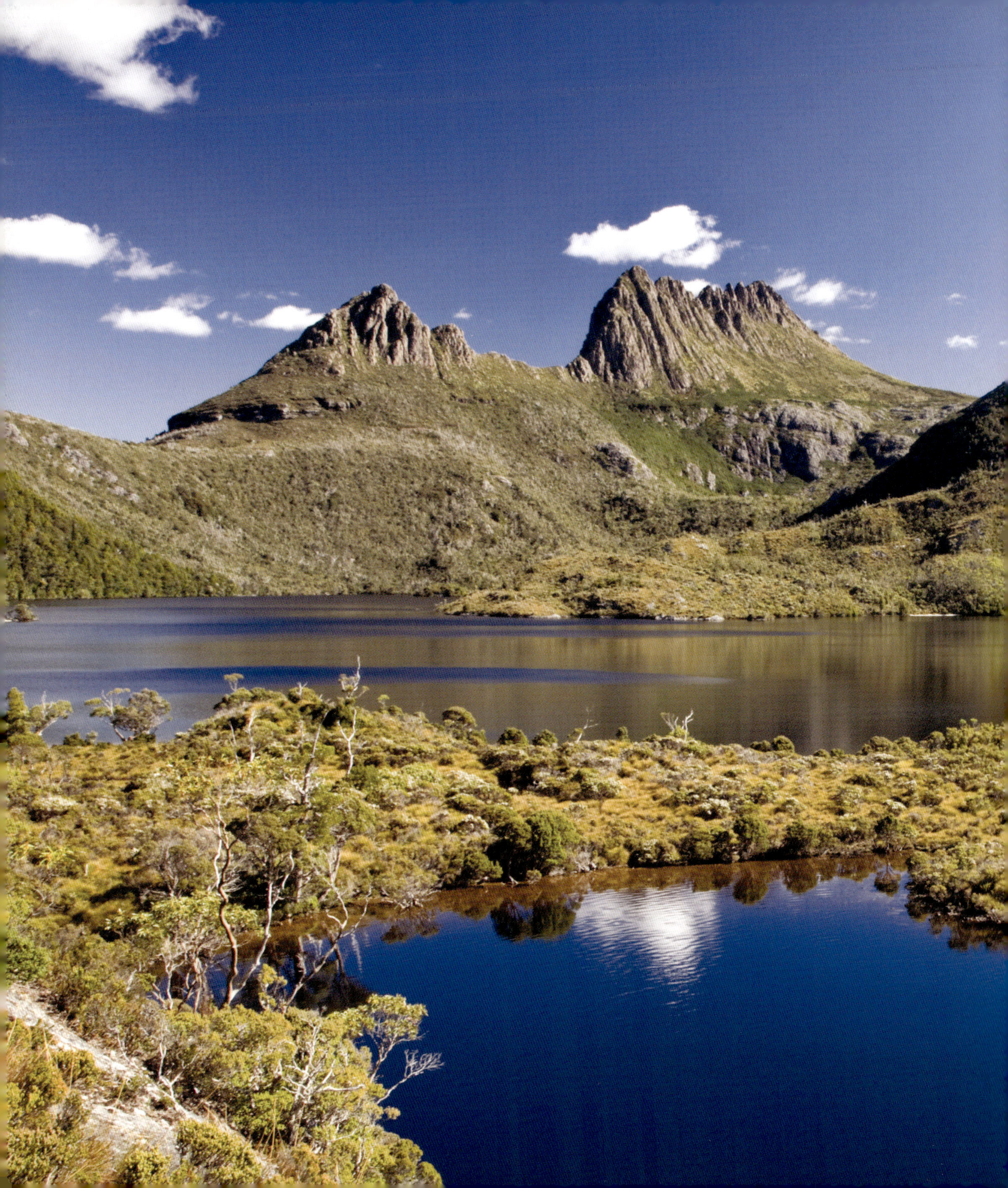

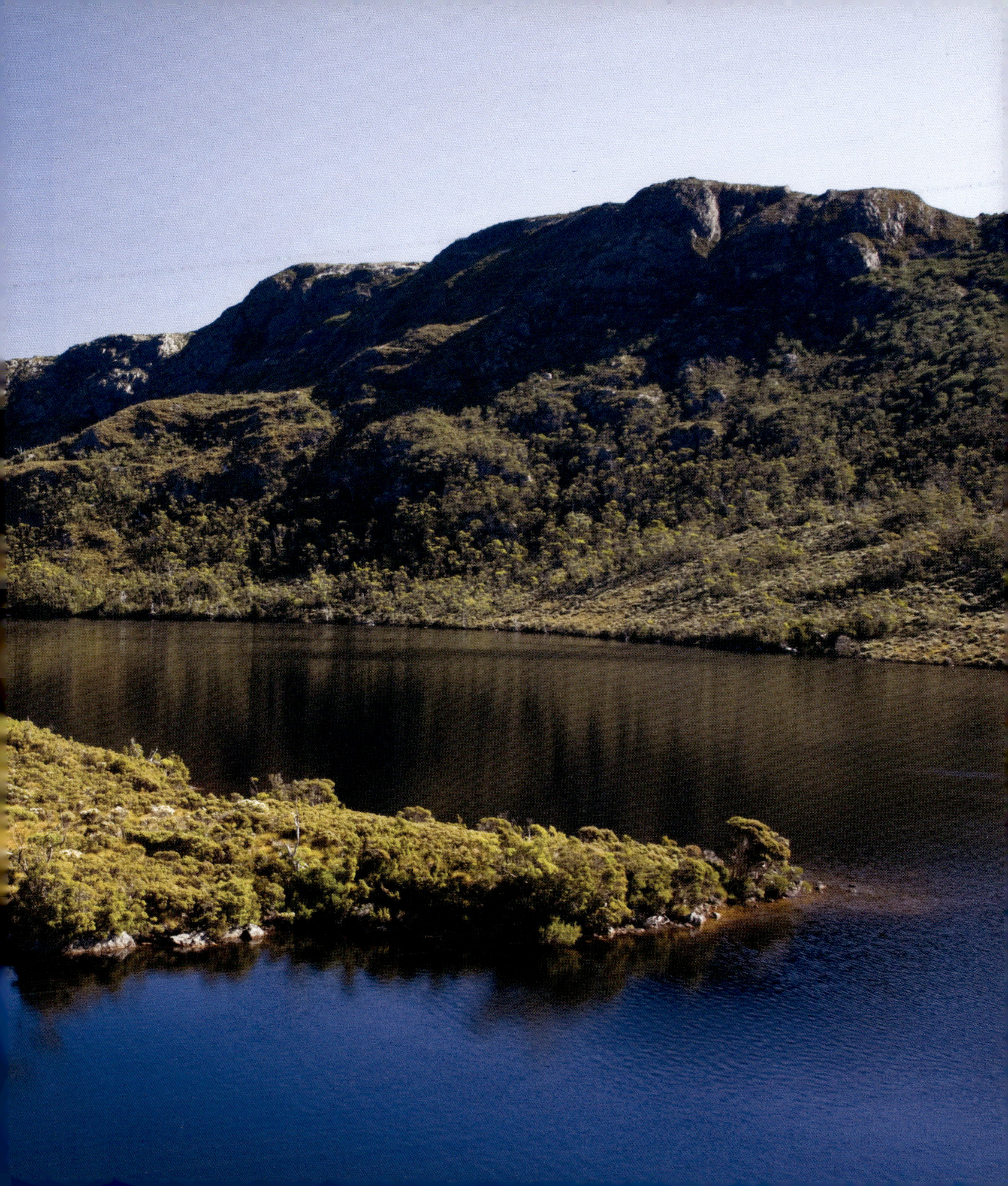

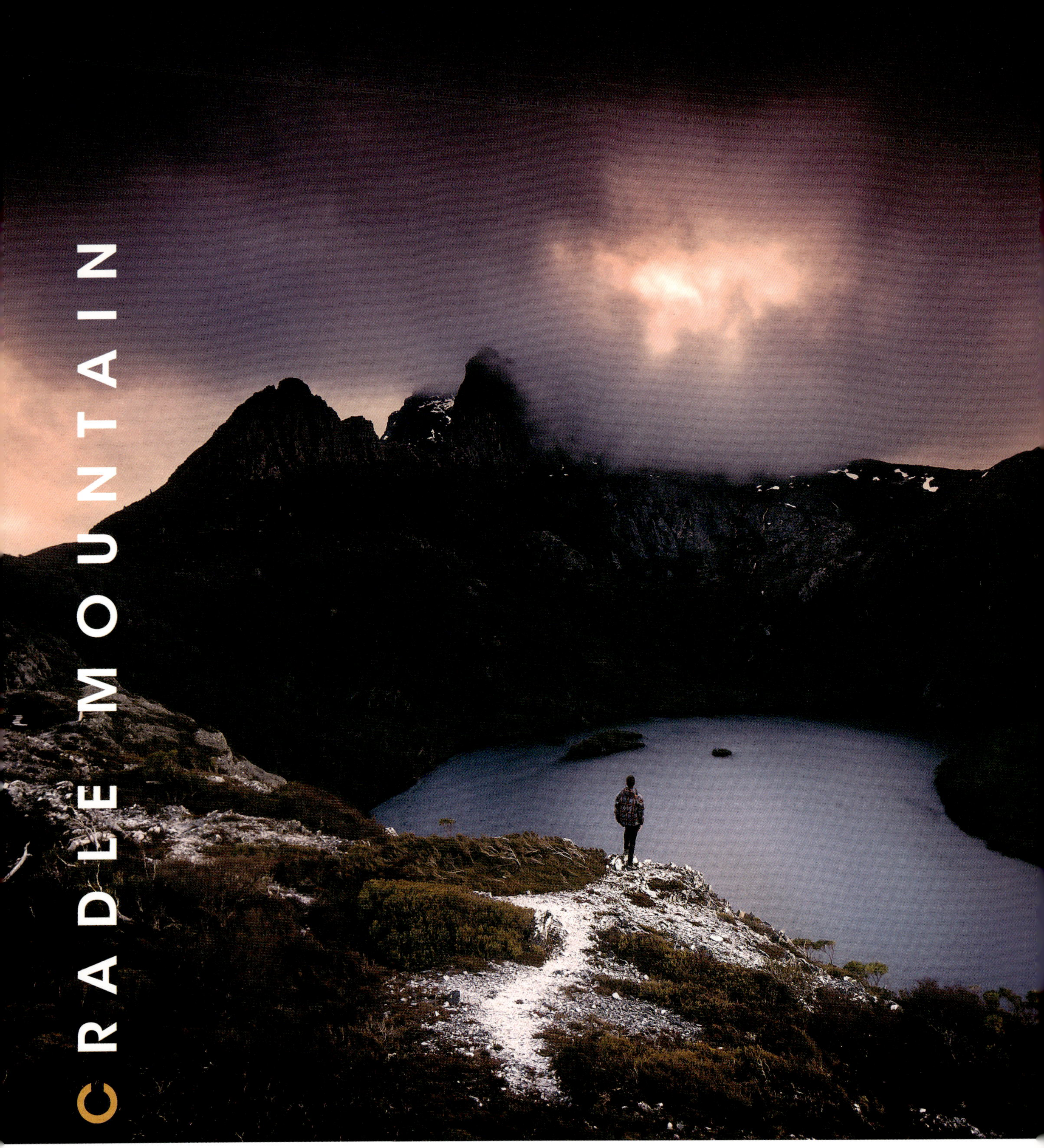
CRADLE MOUNTAIN

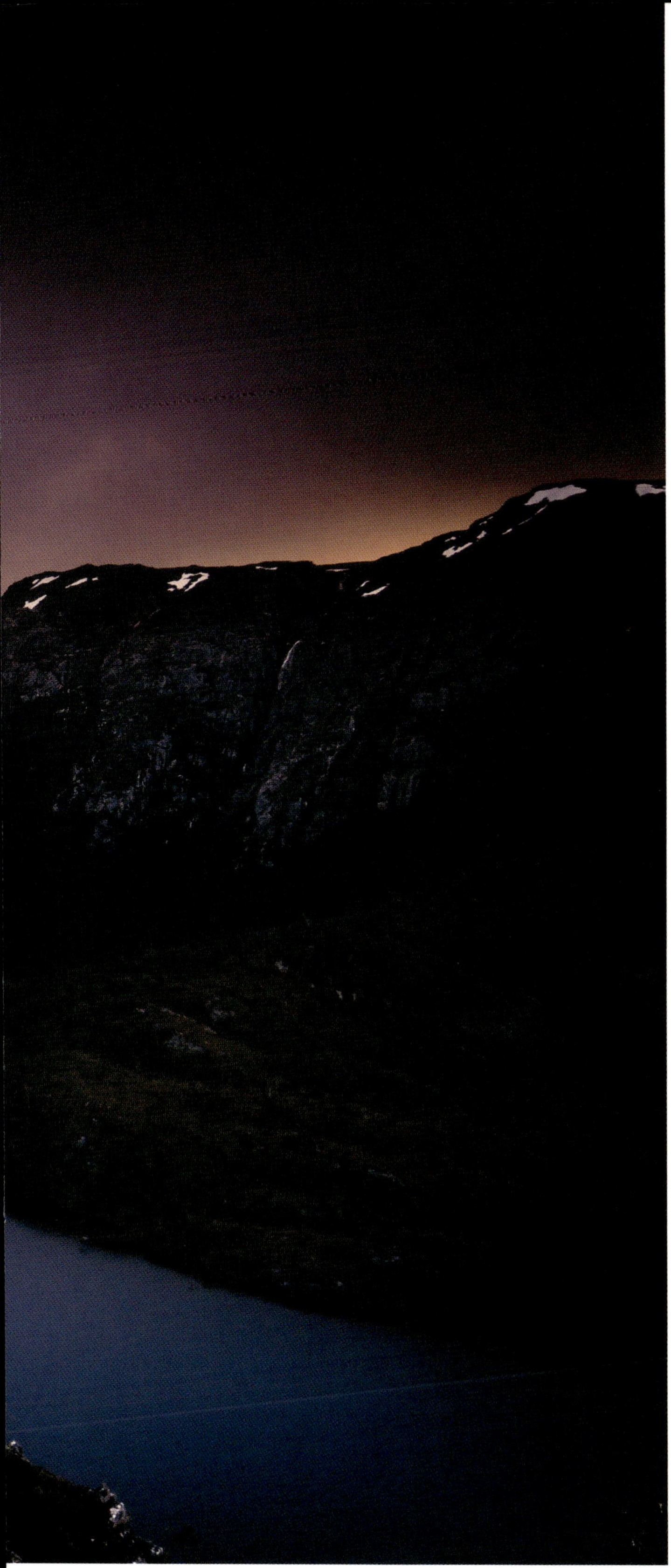

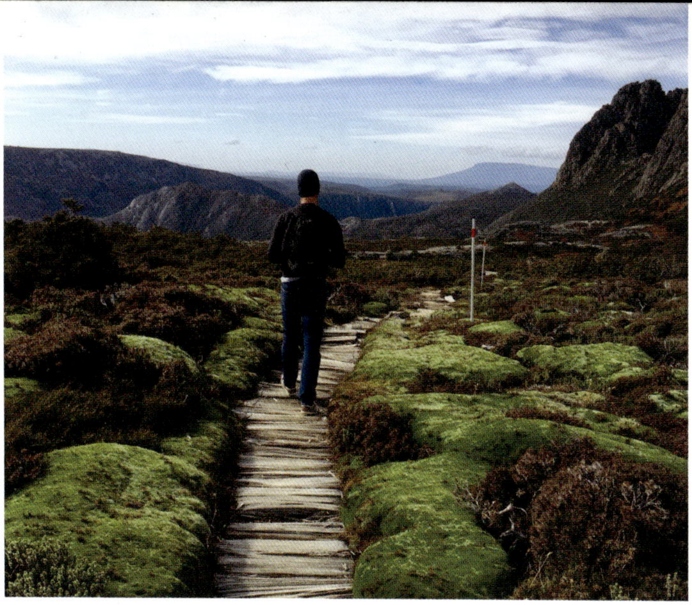

Previous page: Often wearing a balaclava of cloud, visitors must be fortunate to see Cradle Mountain on a clear day.

Left: Cradle Mountain in foreboding winter mode.

Above: The visitor centre provides a guide to short walks, including the classic Dove Lake circuit (6 km, two hours) which stays close to the shore of the lake and covers easy terrain. For a more adventurous walk take the upper circuit – it climbs to Marion's Lookout then passes just below Cradle Mountain on the way to Hanson's Peak before descending back to the Lake Dove carpark (5 hrs) but you'll need to be well equipped with clothing for all weather and snacks to keep you going.

Cradle Mountain is justly famous for its jagged dolerite peaks reflected in beautiful Dove Lake below, and despite the crowds who flock to see it, it remains a magical area and a must-see. One of the few areas of Tasmania's alpine country that can be accessed by car, it still feels very remote and wild when you stand on a high ridge braced against the wind or wander in a hushed mossy forest hung with lichen. Try and stay a few days so you have the time to explore the many walking tracks, stumble across a grazing wombat or snuggle by the fire in the lodge when the weather closes in. Cradle Mountain sits at the northern end of the Cradle Mountain-Lake St Clair National Park and is part of the Wilderness World Heritage Area. The park's ancient rainforest, spiky mountains, alpine moorland, glacial lakes and rare Gondwanan flora and fauna make for a unique and spectacular wilderness.

OVERLAND TRACK

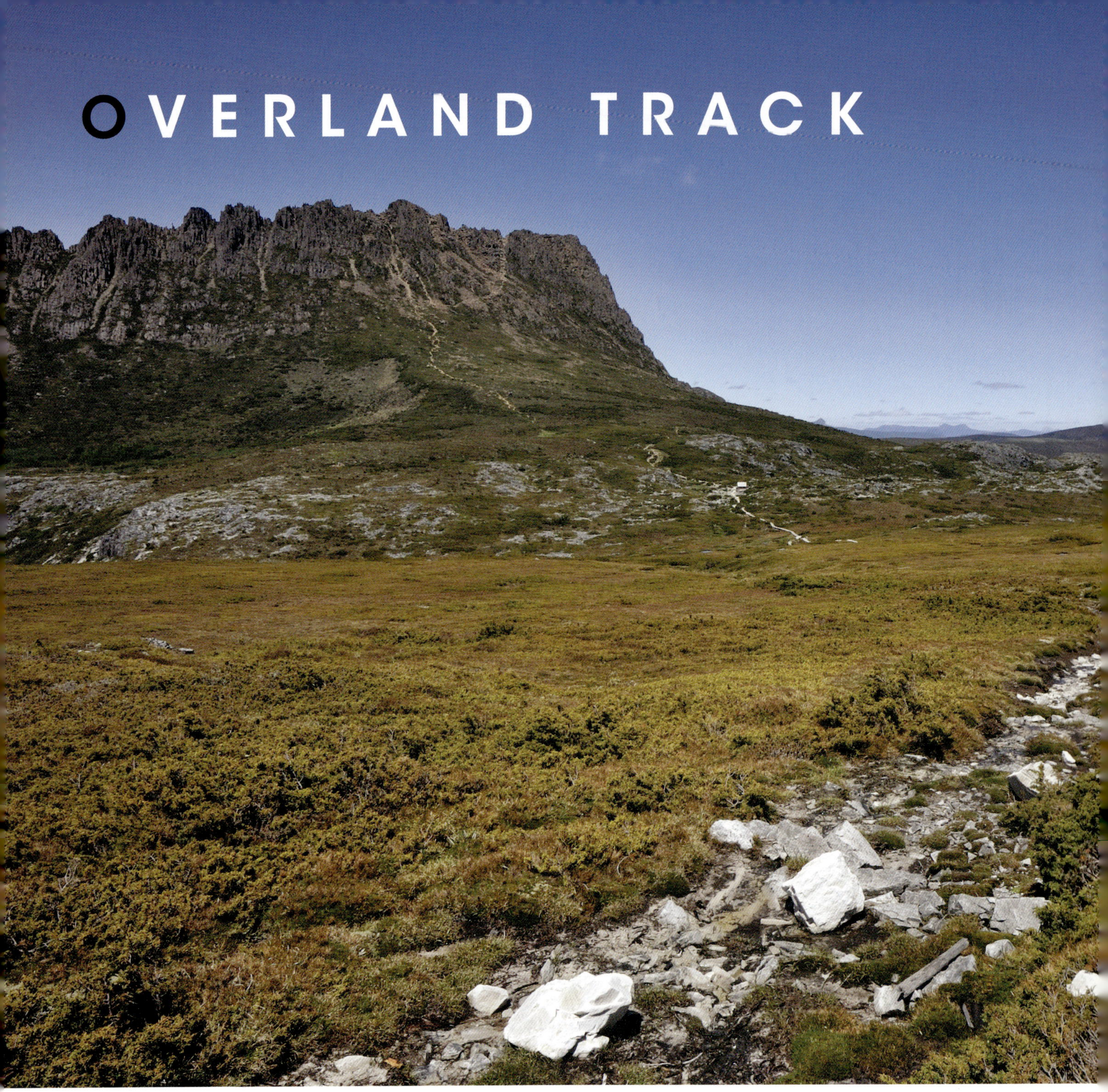

■ Above: There are a few ways to do this walk – self guided and carrying all your own gear and sleeping in a tent or basic hut in all weather conditions. Guided and catered but staying in tents, or carrying just your clothes and sleeping in comfortable huts with hot showers and gourmet meals on the Cradle Mountain Huts Walk.

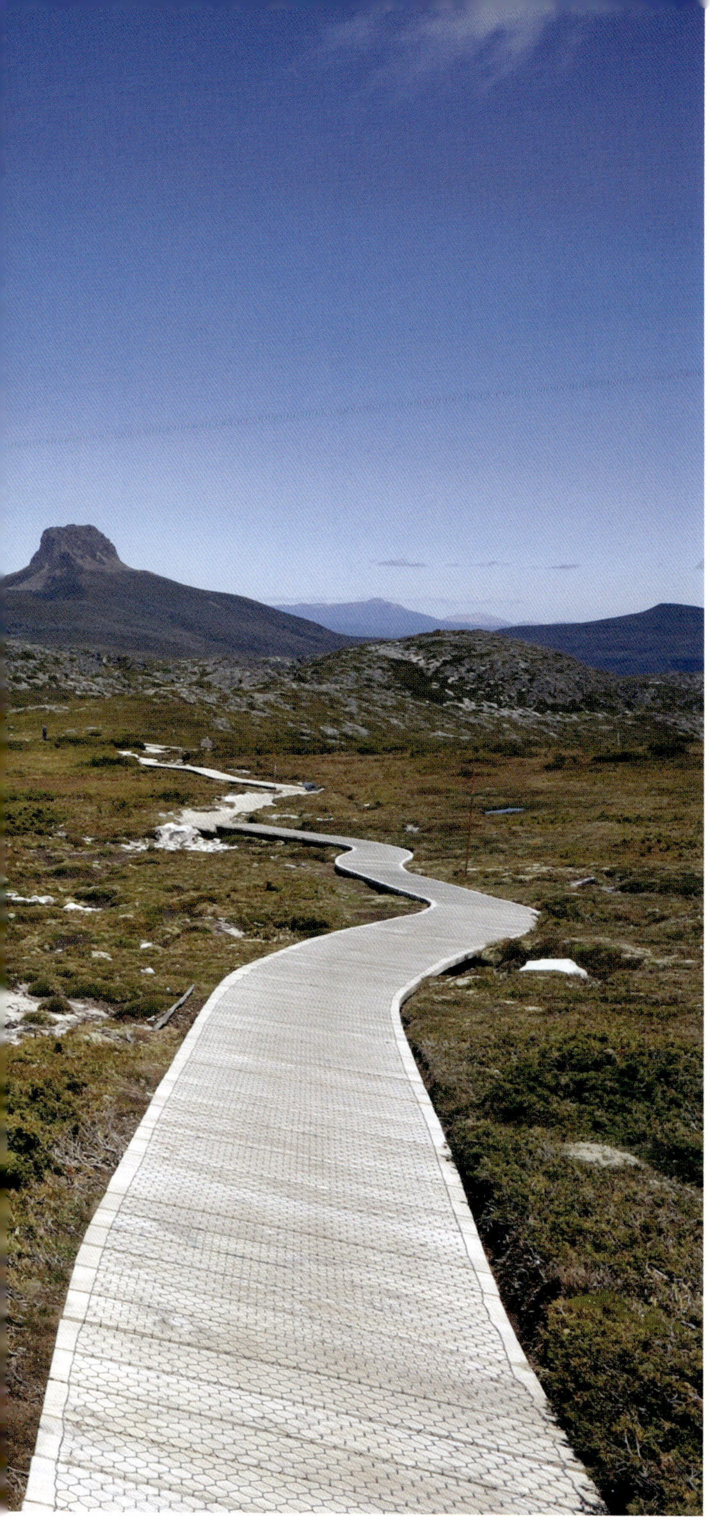

This is the classic Tasmanian walk, through an area of alpine wilderness unlike any other in Australia. The six-day Overland Track is about 65 km from Dove Lake to Lake St Clair, and traverses a high plateau in the heart of the island, scoured and shaped by ice ages. In every direction lie distinctive and unusual mountain peaks and ranges, sheer columns and cliffs of dark dolerite. The side trips on this walk rival the attractions of the main track, including a route up Mt Ossa (1617 m), Tasmania's highest mountain, and exploring them can extend the trip by several days. The track winds through a varied landscape of open moorland, glacial tarns and rainforests of myrtle, deciduous beech and sassafras. There are also streams and waterfalls, stands of snow gums and native pines and flowering heath. It's one of the world's great walks and an unforgettable experience. Of course, in the mountains it can snow at any time of year so walkers must be prepared for all conditions. The walking season is October to May. Bookings and serious planning are required so check the Parks & Wildlife Service website for more information.

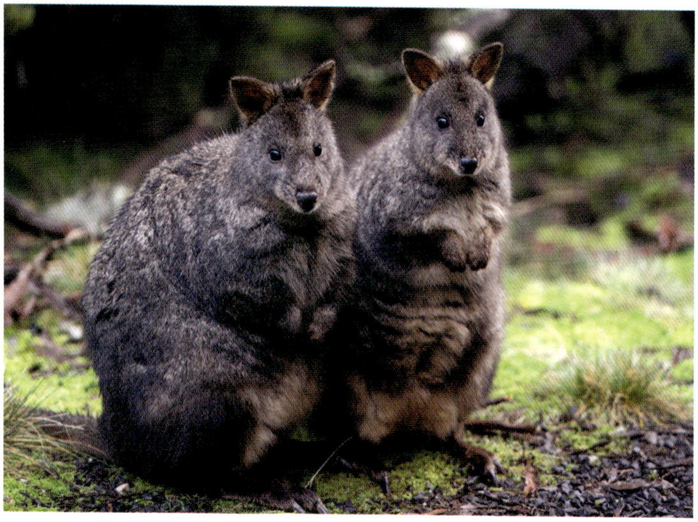

■ Right: The stocky pademelon has short legs and tail to help it move through dense vegetation and is often seen in the Cradle Mountain-Lake St Clair National Park.

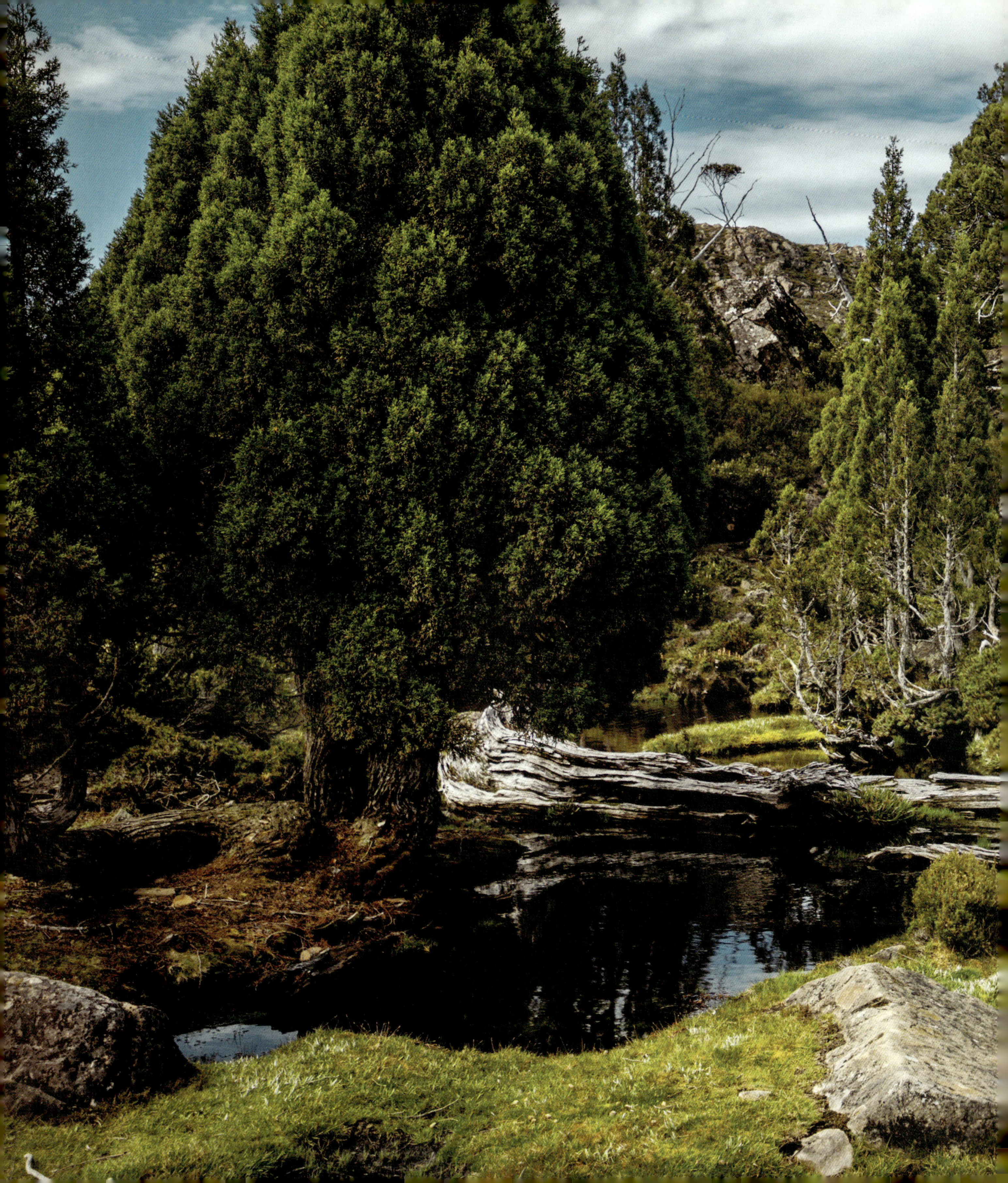

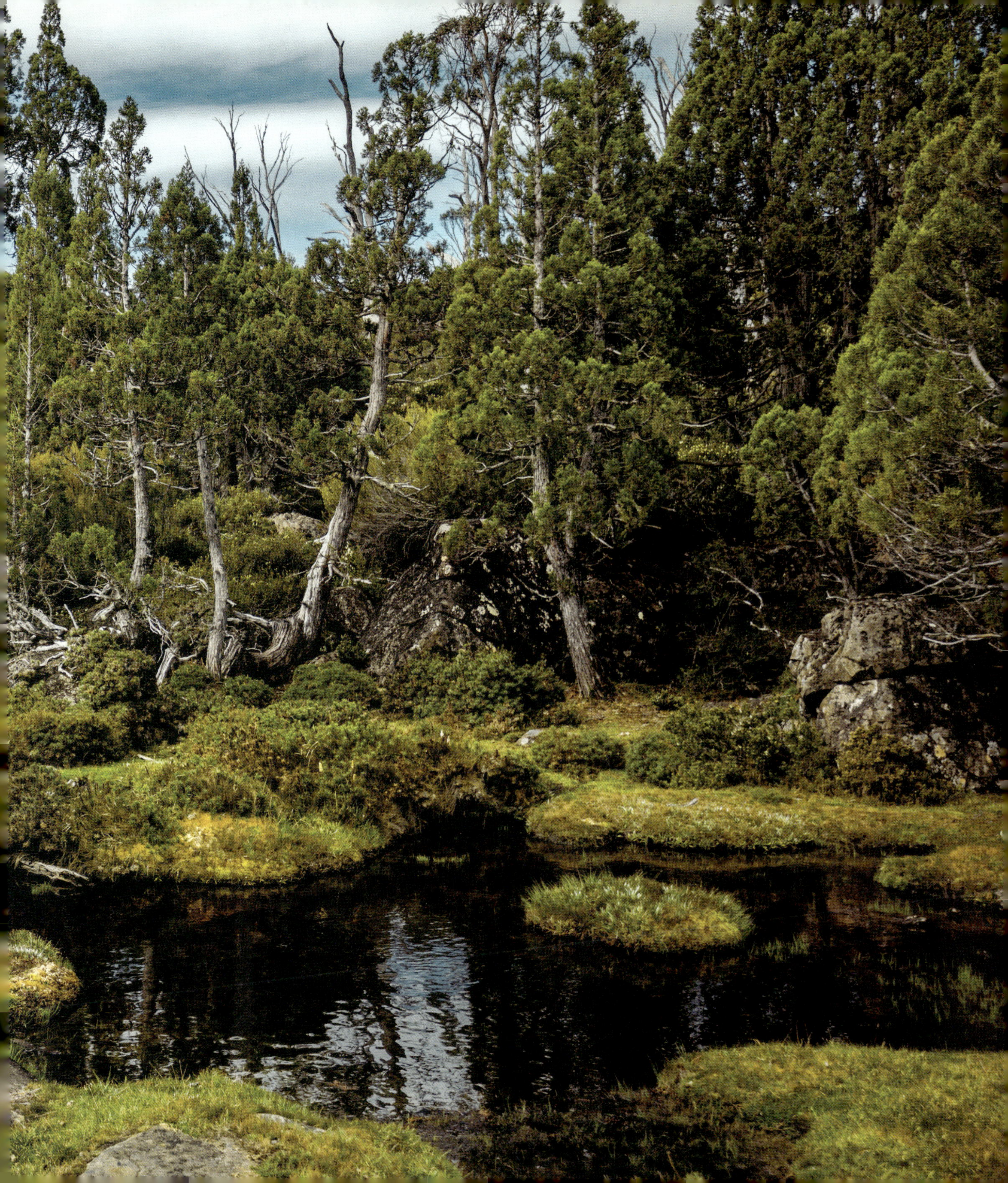

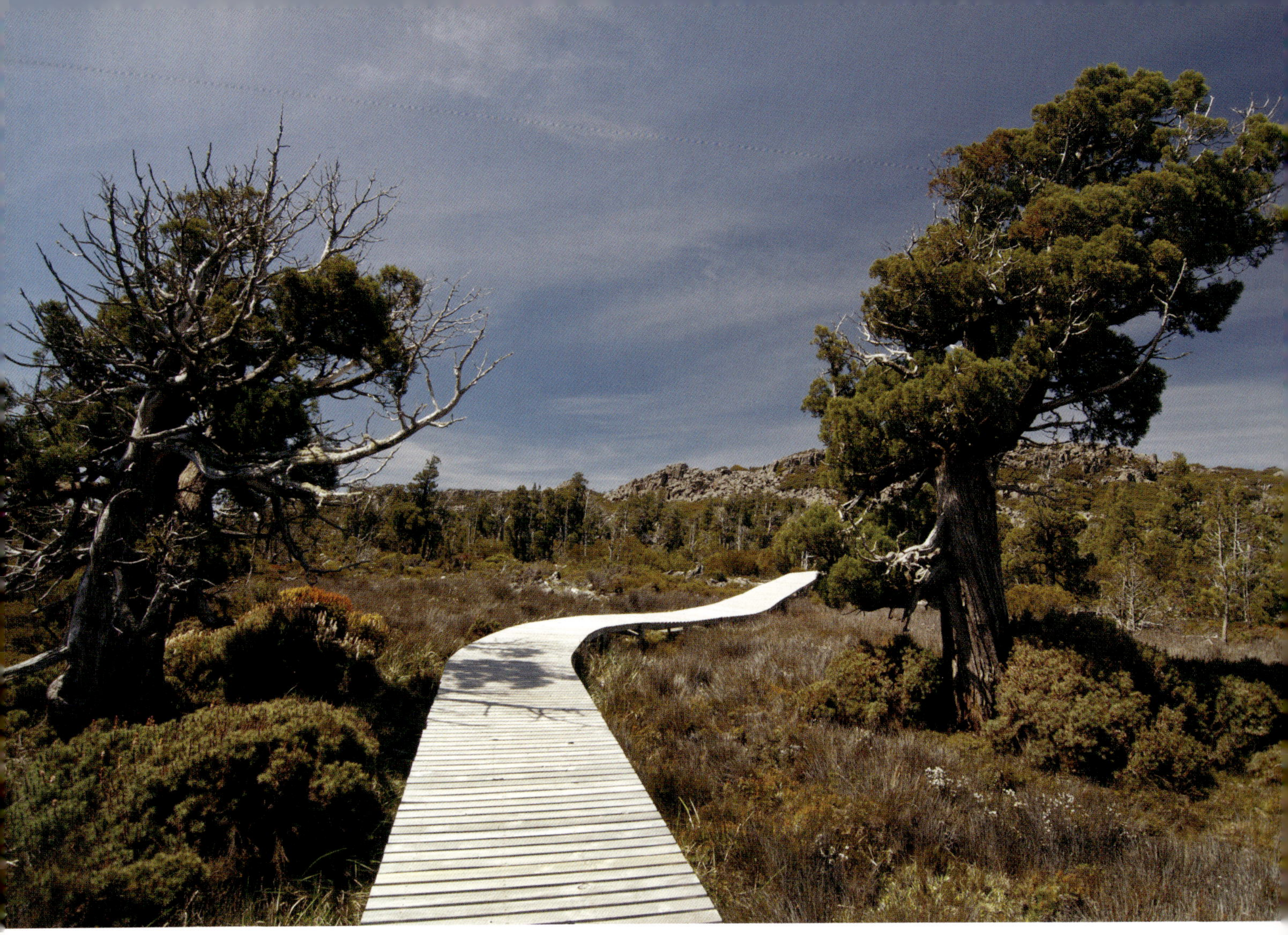

CENTRAL PLATEAU

There are just two routes running north to south through the middle of Tasmania. The easterly route, the Midland Highway, runs through the well-preserved and picturesque Georgian garrison towns of Oatlands, Ross and Campbell Town. This is a route for those interested in architecture, convict history and plentiful refreshments. The westerly route via Bothwell is slower but it's a spectacular drive through the kilometre-high Central Plateau Conservation Area. The plateau has been scraped fairly flat by a succession of glaciers that have left it dotted with hundreds of lakes teeming with wild rainbow trout, making it a popular destination for anglers. Miena, on the shore of Great Lake, is little more than a lonely settlement of fishing shacks. Past the northern edge of the lake, the landscape is inhospitable and barren. Swept by intensely cold westerly winds, it's nevertheless rich in rare alpine plants and animals. At Pine Lake you can stop and walk the Pencil Pine boardwalk (600 m) to see these gnarled native conifers and cushion plants, before the road descends a gap in the Great Western Tiers to Golden Valley and Deloraine on the plains below.

■ Previous page: Pools of Bethesda in Walls of Jerusalem National Park. The park encloses an area of the Central Plateau that contains over 4000 lakes and tarns within about 480 sq km. The 'walls' are five peaks surrounding a basin. To enter, walkers must pass through the 'gates' of the old city – Herods, Damascus, Zion, Jaffa and Ephraims. The twisted pencil pines and snow gums bear witness to the harsh conditions of this alpine wilderness. There is no access by road and walkers must be prepared for extreme conditions.

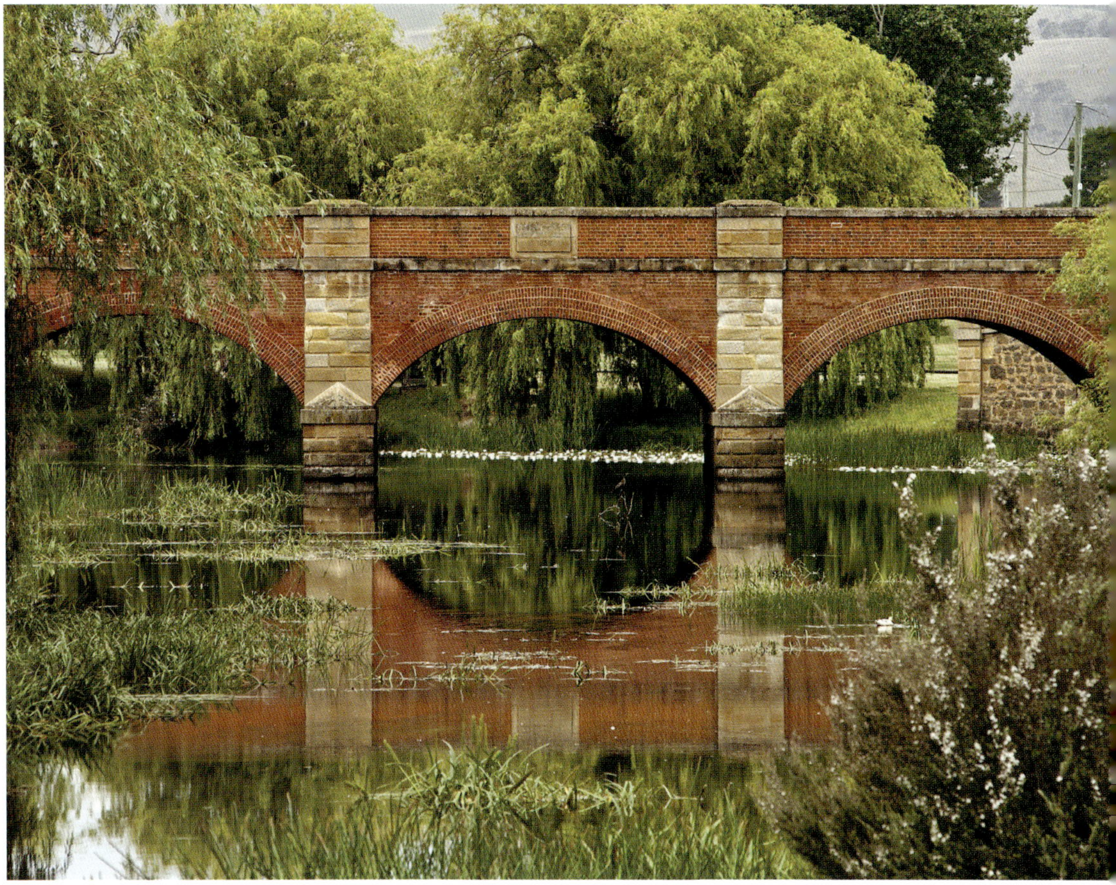

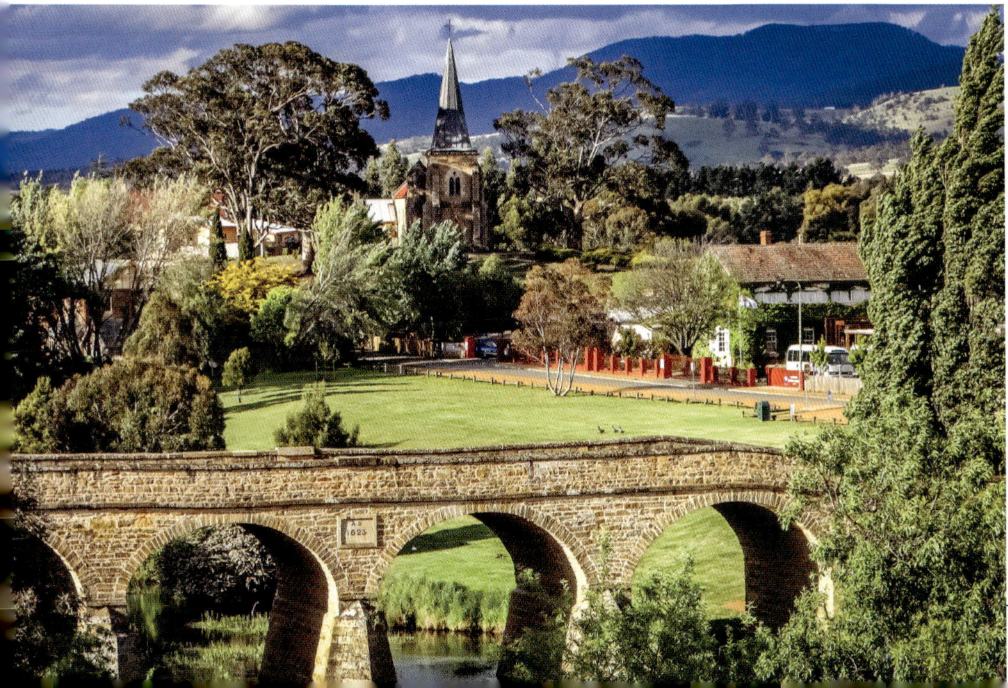

Opposite page: Pencil Pines live in sub alpine environments, above 800 m, and can live more than 1200 years.

Above: The Red Bridge in Campbell Town on the Midland Highway, the gentle route through central Tasmania. It was built by convicts in 1838 using one and a half million bricks handmade in the town itself.

Left: Richmond Bridge, 26 km north-east of Hobart. Built by convicts in 1823, it is the oldest stone span bridge in Australia still in use.

NORTH WEST

Lacking a famous attraction such as Cradle Mountain or Port Arthur, the north west is less visited than other parts of the state but this is precisely the appeal of this beautiful off-the-beaten-track corner of Tasmania. A string of small towns lie on the north coast, such as the picturesque village of Stanley tucked under its curious promontory, 'The Nut'. The west coast is pounded relentlessly by howling gales and violent seas, but also boasts the cleanest air in the world at Cape Grim. At Marrawah, the massive waves host an annual surf competition and heading south, the Arthur-Pieman Conservation Area protects countless Aboriginal archaeological sites including middens, hut sites and rock engravings. At the mouth of the Arthur river, it is possible to see the wild and fierce beauty of this coast with its weather-sculpted rocks and beaches littered with logs, and then cruise upstream into a silent, black and pristine river bordered by rainforest. From here you can drive south on the unsealed and winding Western Explorer route to Corinna and Strahan, or west into the Tarkine rainforest.

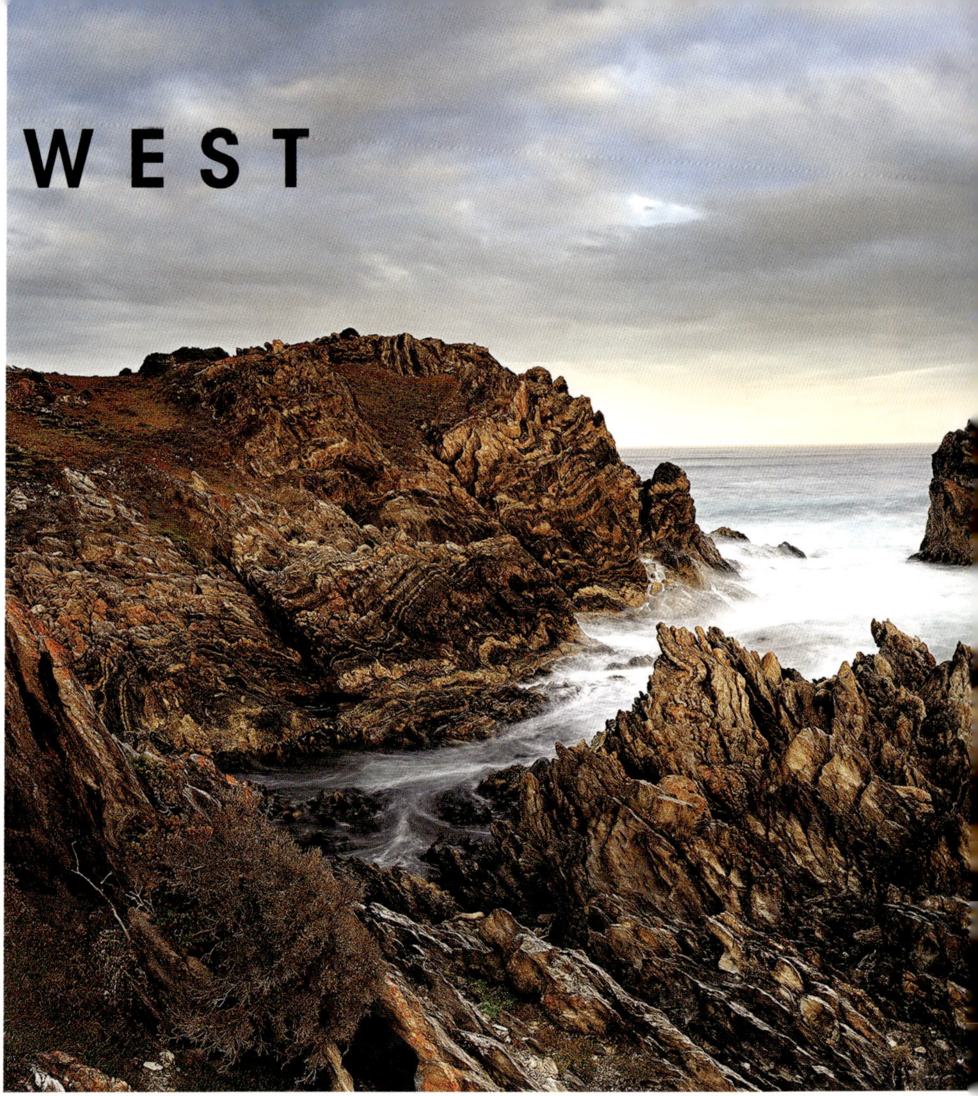

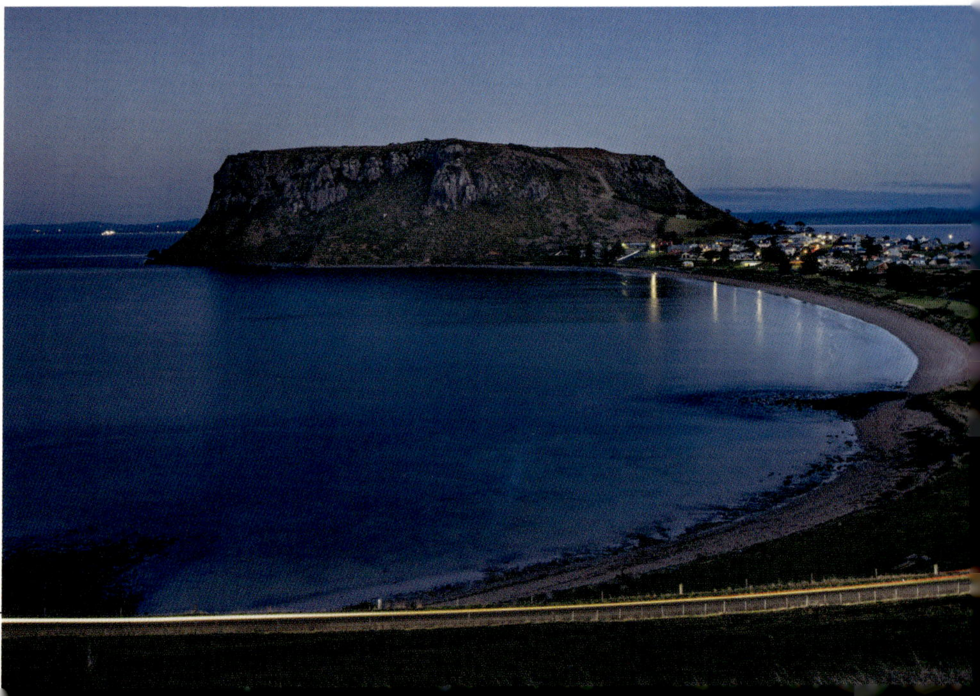

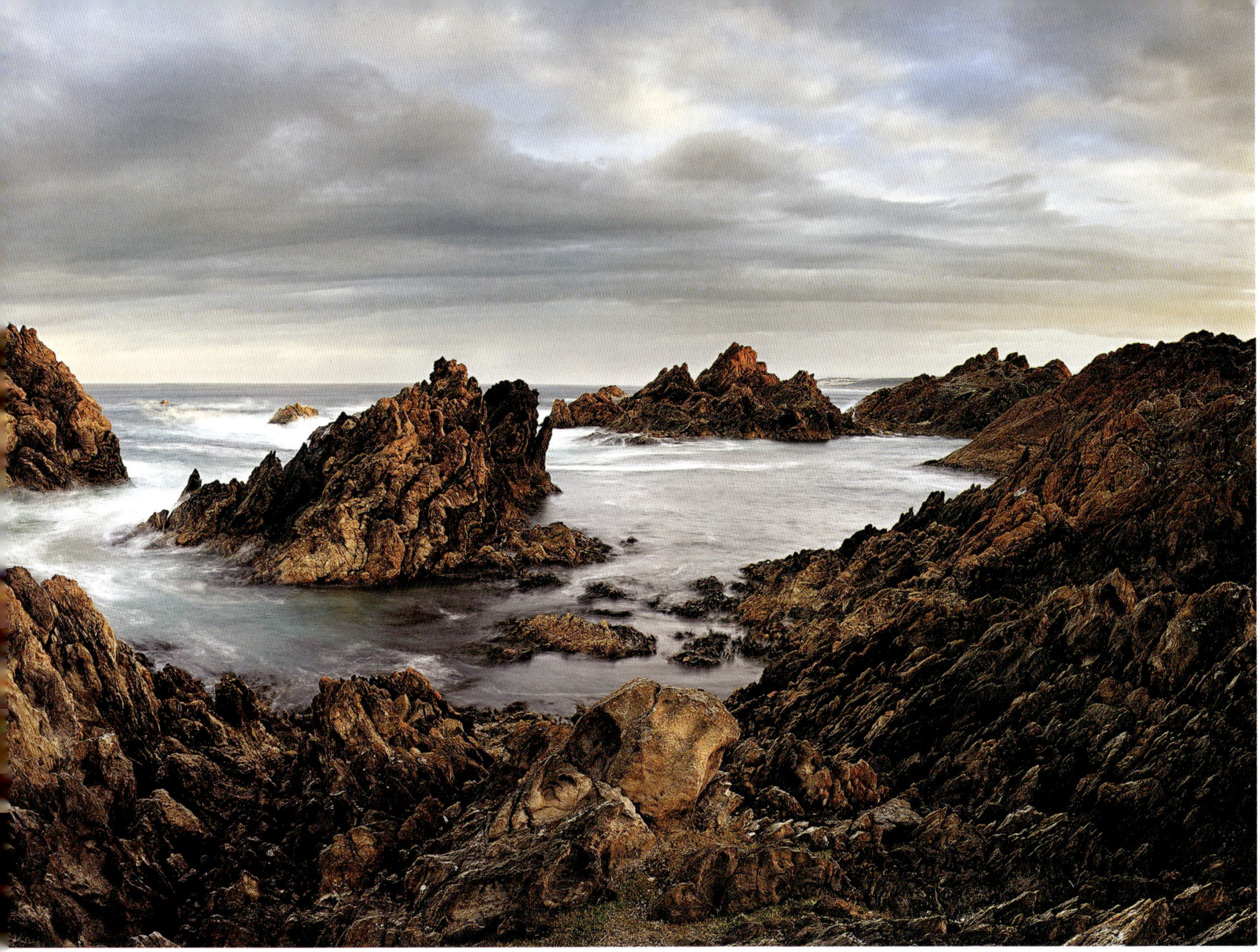

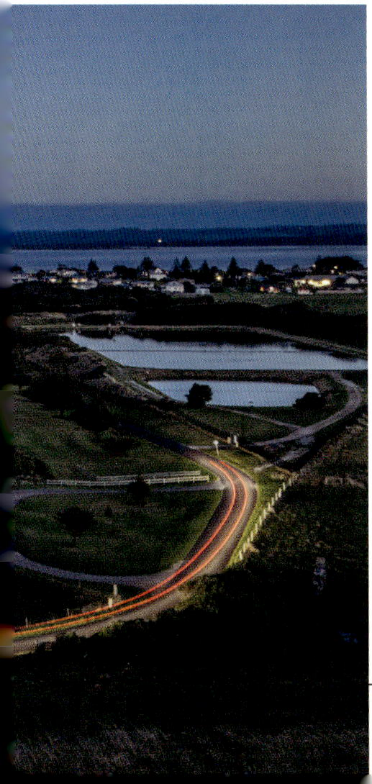

Above: Rupert Point, near the mouth of the Pieman River. Explore this dramatic coastline by walking all or some of the Arthur River Coast Walk from Arthur River Bridge to Bluff Hill Lighthouse (16 km return, 4-5 hours). There are also short walks at Sundown Point and Couta Rocks.

Left: The town of Stanley nestled under the Nut at dusk. This is one of Tasmania's oldest towns, the early headquarters of the Van Diemens Land Company, and it has a fine collection of Georgian and Victorian architecture. It's a 20 minute climb to the top of the Nut where there is a 45 minute circuit walk.

TARKINE

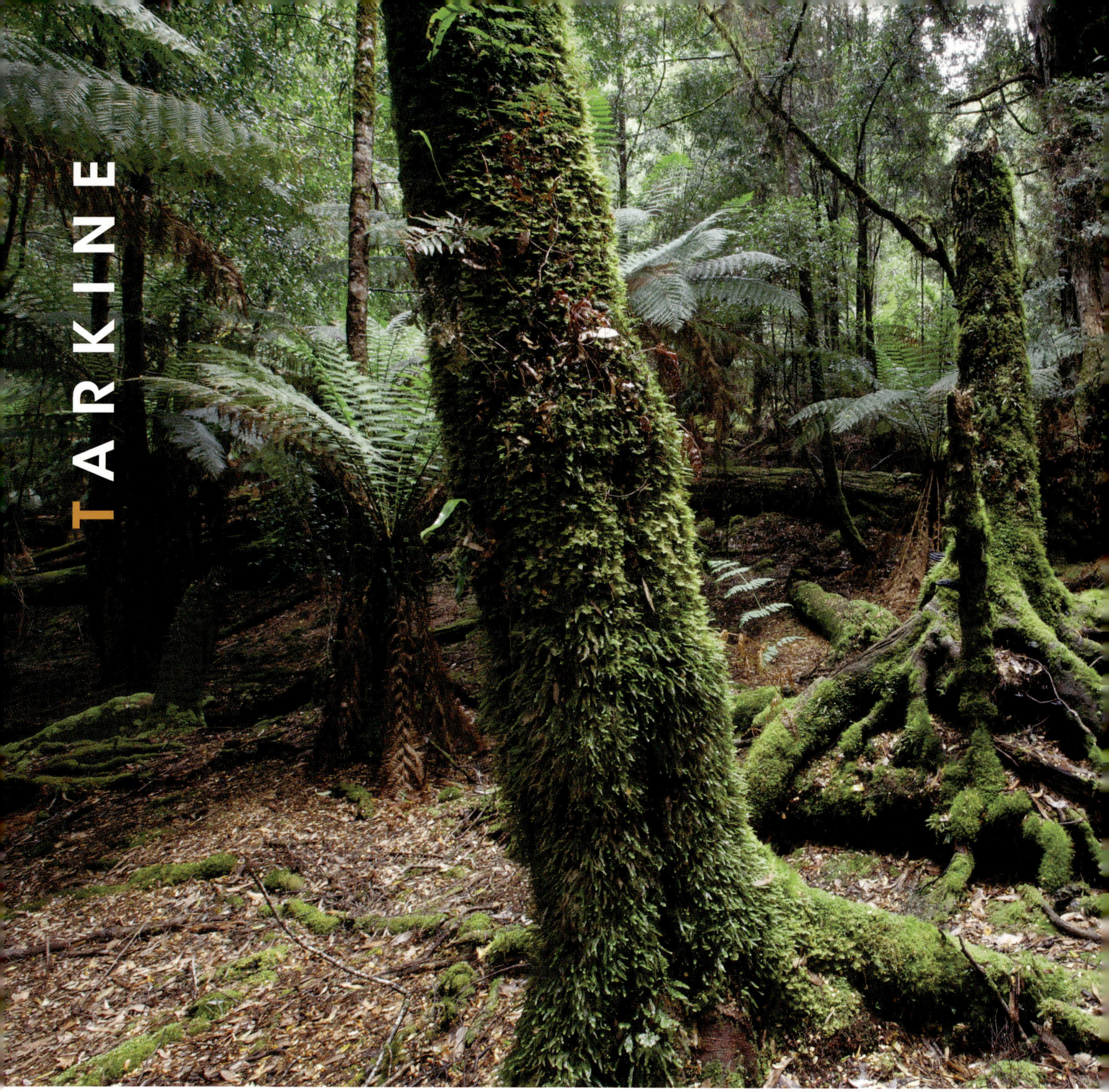

■ Above: The best way to experience the Tarkine is to take a multi-day walk with expert guides, like the Tarkine Rainforest Walk with Tarkine Trails, but you can also access the northern edge by taking the Tarkine Drive, where there are good short rainforest walks and lookouts at Trowutta, Milkshake Hills, Lake Chisholm and Sumac Lookout.

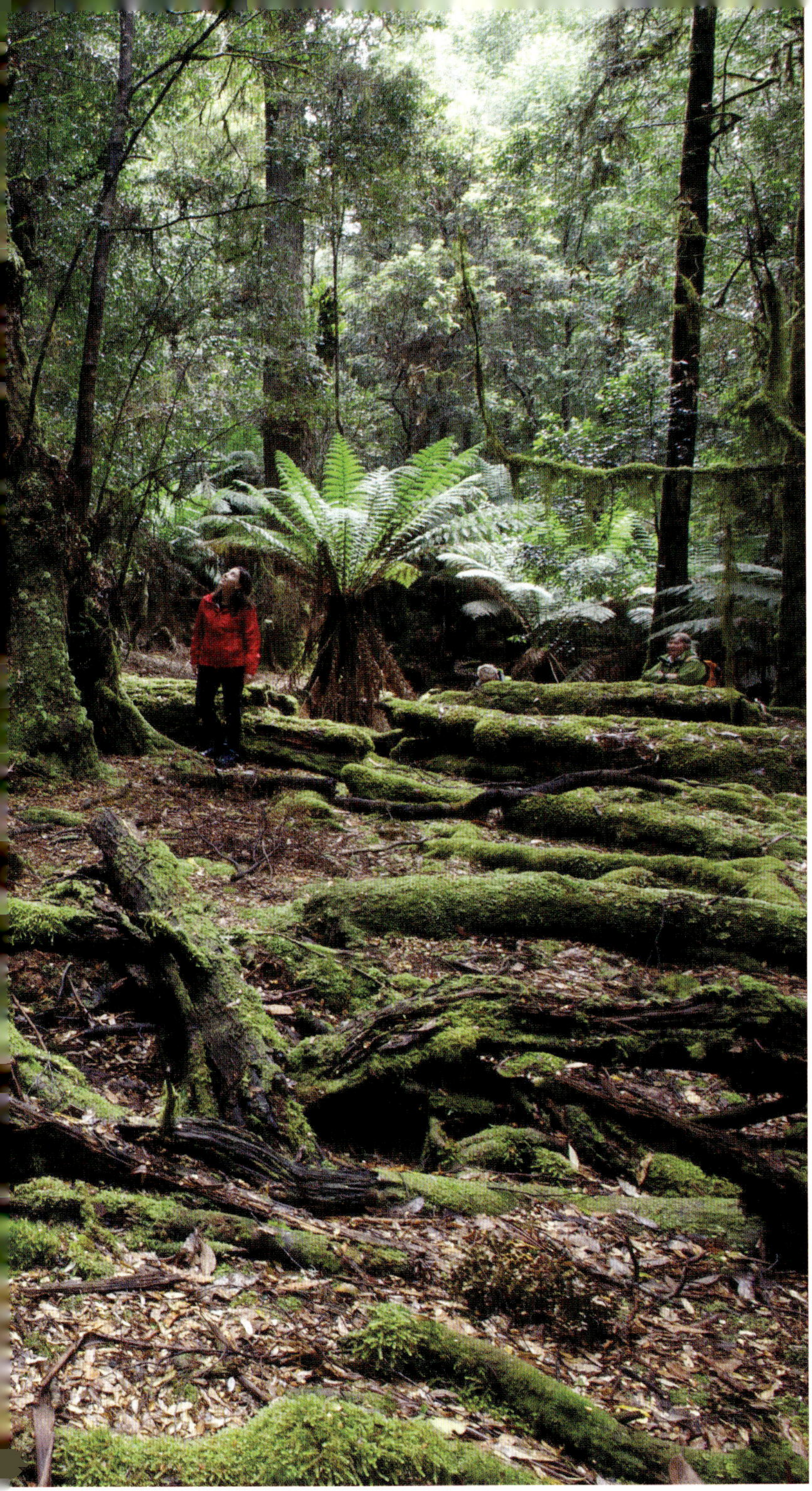

The Tarkine is a little mysterious. It's not a national park or reserve but it includes the Savage River National Park, the Arthur-Pieman Conservation Area and several Forest Reserves. This vast remote region of wild forests and rugged coastline encompasses 447,000 hectares and Australia's largest tract of temperate rainforest. The Tarkine is bound by the Arthur River to the north, the Pieman River to the south, the Murchison Highway to the east and the Southern Ocean. Its forests of myrtle, sassafras and leatherwood are home to many plants and animals not found anywhere else in the world, such as the Tasmanian devil and perhaps even the legendary Thylacine, or Tasmanian Tiger, officially extinct since 1936. The Tarkine's bright green mossy damp depths, enormous ancient trees and abundant rivers have visitors feeling moved and inspired. Named after the Tarkiner people, one of three Aboriginal groups who lived in the north west, the Tarkine is also a rich source of archeological artefacts that reveal much about the life and culture of its original inhabitants. Conservationists are campaigning for the area to be protected from logging and mining by national park or world heritage listing.

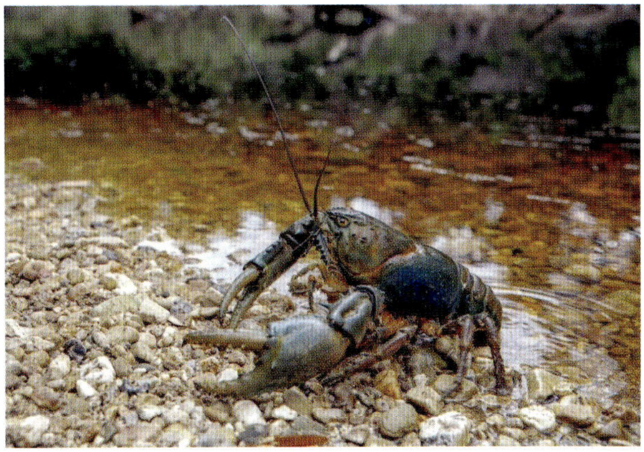

■ Right: The giant freshwater crayfish is an extraordinary creature found only in Tasmania. It grows up to a metre long and weighs up to 5 kilos. The biggest freshwater invertebrate on our planet, the crayfish takes 40 years to grow to full size and can live for 60 years. The mossy mud turrets seen on Tarkine tracks are built by the crayfish to protect its burrows.

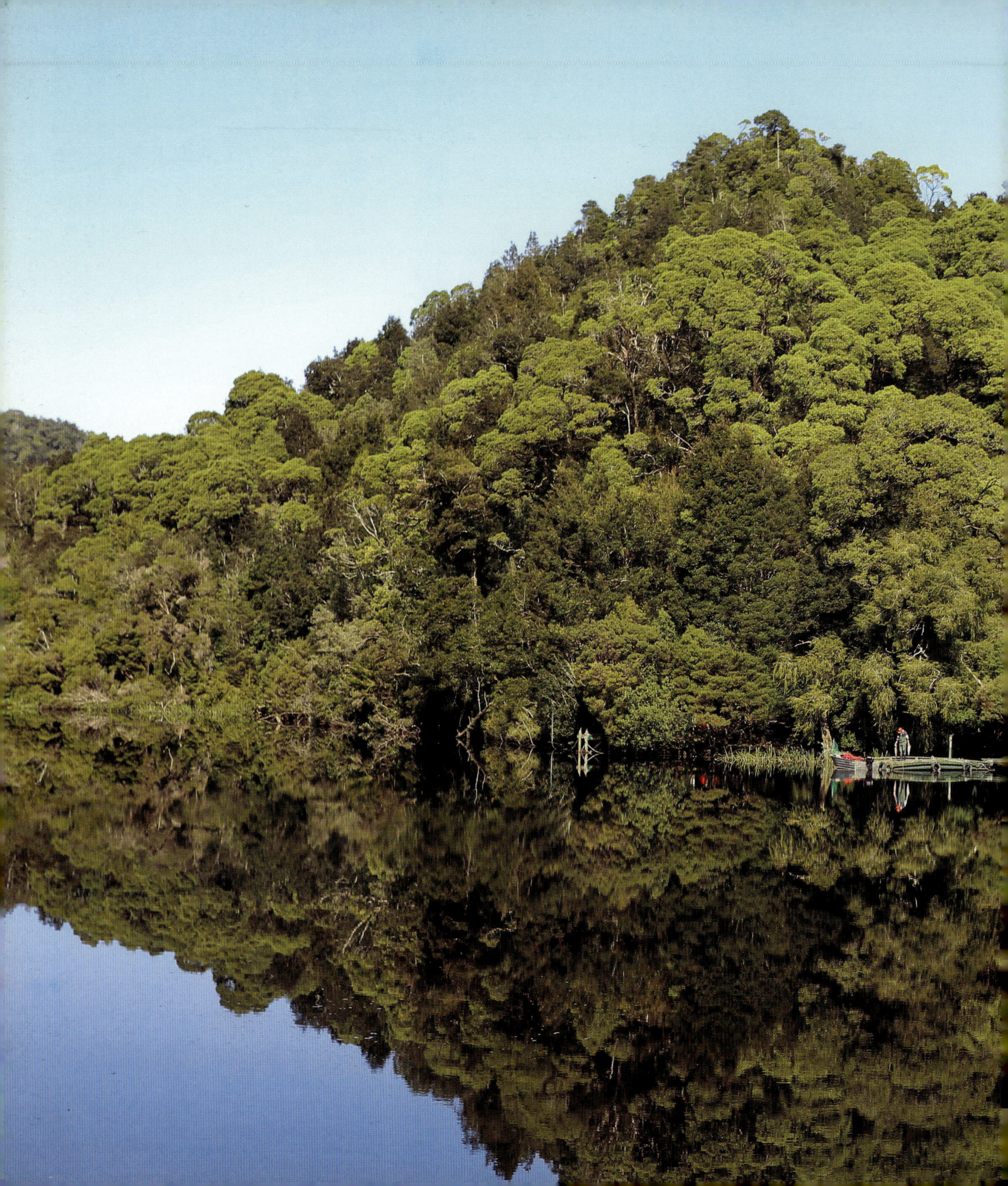

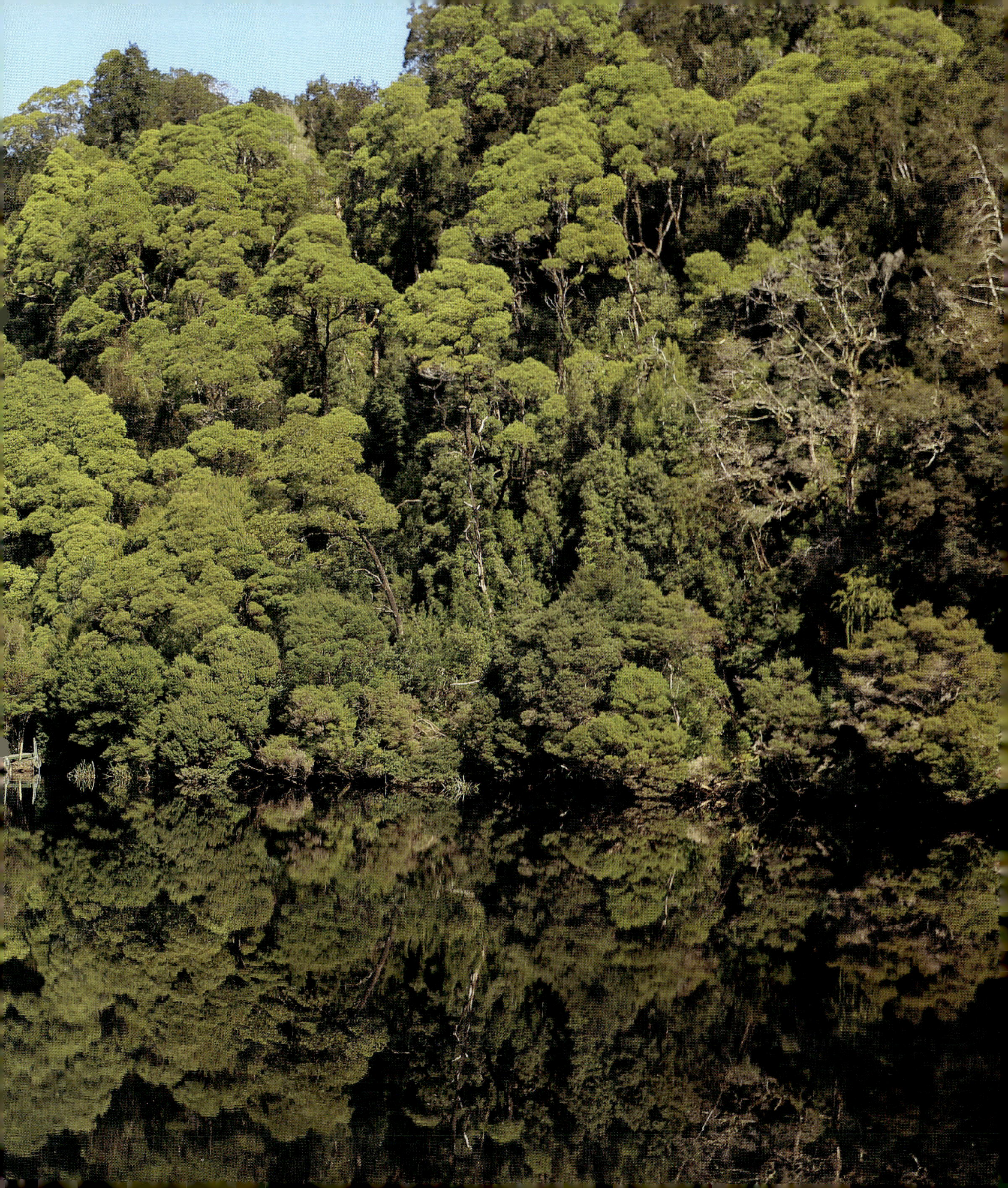

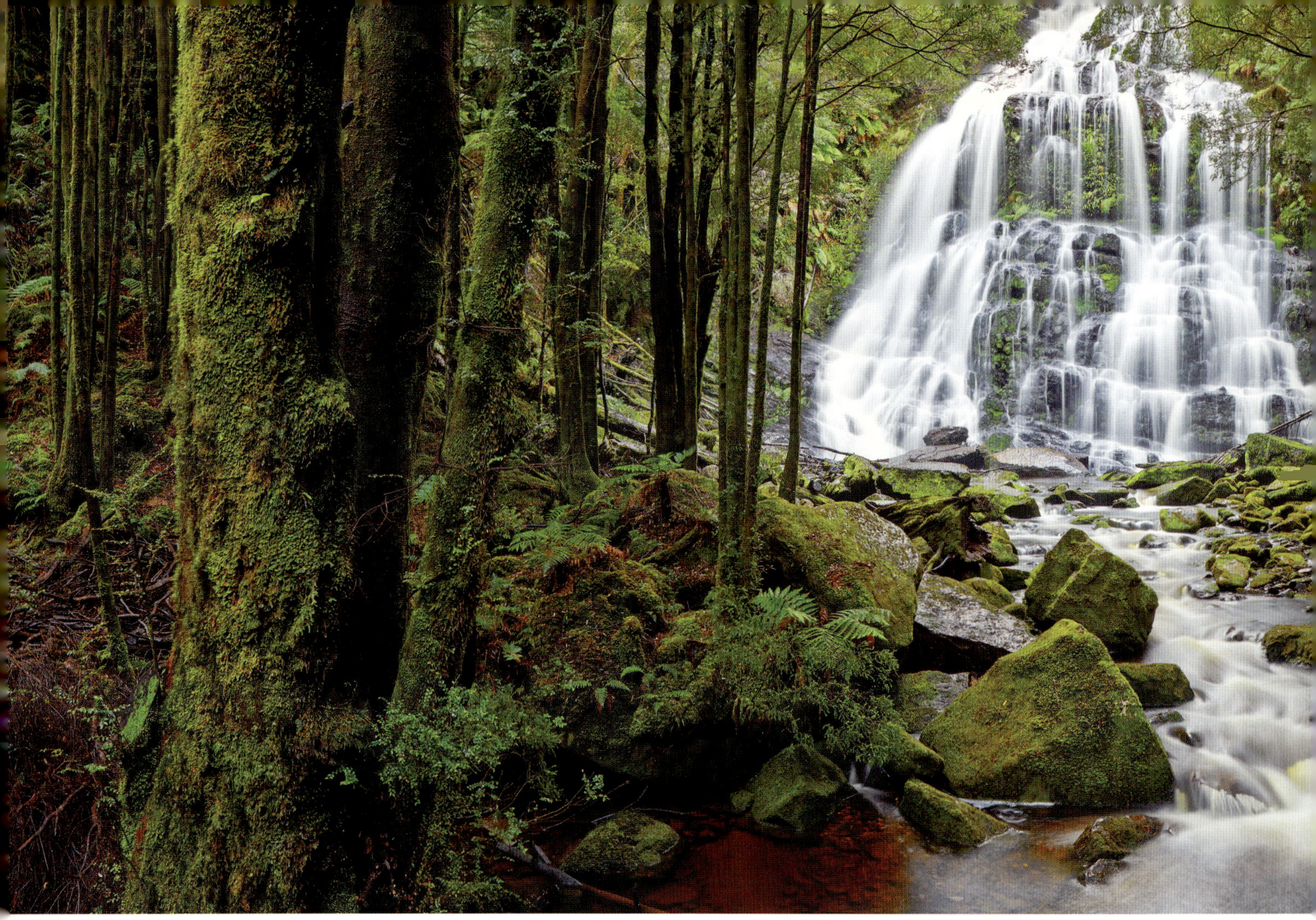

FRANKLIN-GORDON

The Franklin-Gordon Wild Rivers National Park lies in the heart of the Tasmanian Wilderness World Heritage Area. Its rugged ravines, gorges and wild and pristine rivers are particularly treasured in the state as they were very nearly lost to a hydro-electric dam project in the 1980s. Conservationists blockaded dam workers on the Franklin River and successfully lobbied the federal government to intervene. The Lyell Highway bisects the park and provides access points for rafting trips and walking tracks. The best short walk is Donaghys Hill Wilderness Lookout (40 mins return), an easy walk through forest emerging onto a ridge with incredible views of the Franklin River Valley and Frenchman's Cap (1446 m). There is also a very challenging 4-5 day walk to the summit of this distinctive white quartzite mountain peak. If that's a step too far, you can get to the Franklin River if you walk the first five minutes of the Frenchmans Cap Walking Track or take the Franklin River Nature Trail (1 km circuit). From west coast village Strahan you can take a boat cruise on the tranquil Gordon River, and explore the ruins of the brutal penal settlement of Sarah Island, hemmed in by Hell's Gate – the narrow entrance to Macquarie Harbour.

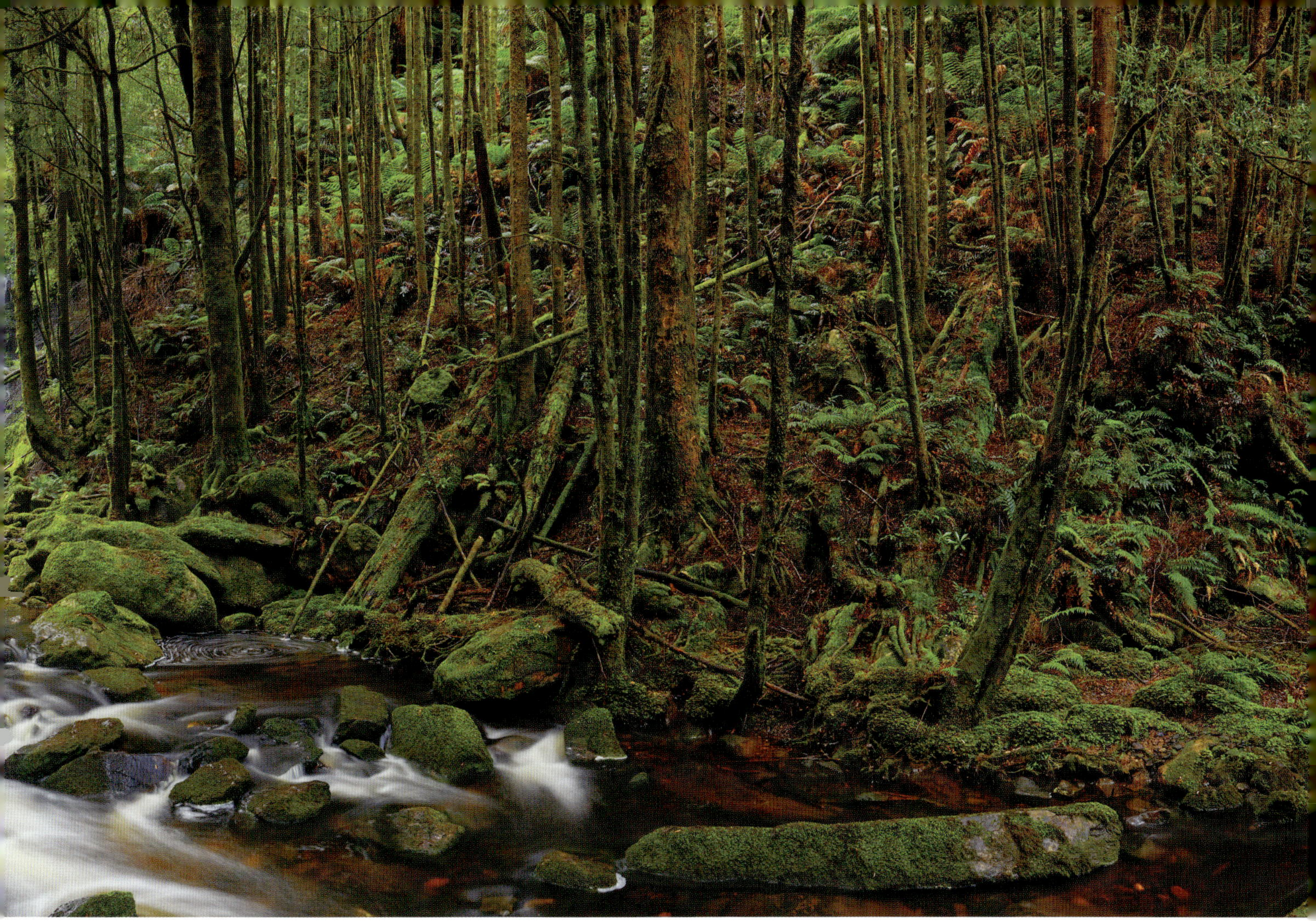

Previous page: Heritage Landing on the lower Gordon River. Gliding along this river's rainforest reflections, the water stained almost black with tannin, is an unmissable experience.

Above: Nelson Falls can be reached via a 1 km boardwalk track through cool temperate rainforest. The trail is just west of Victoria Pass on the Lyell Highway.

Right: Strahan on the west coast, once a mining and timber cutting town, is now the base for a fishing fleet and boats cruising Macquarie Harbour and the Gordon River.

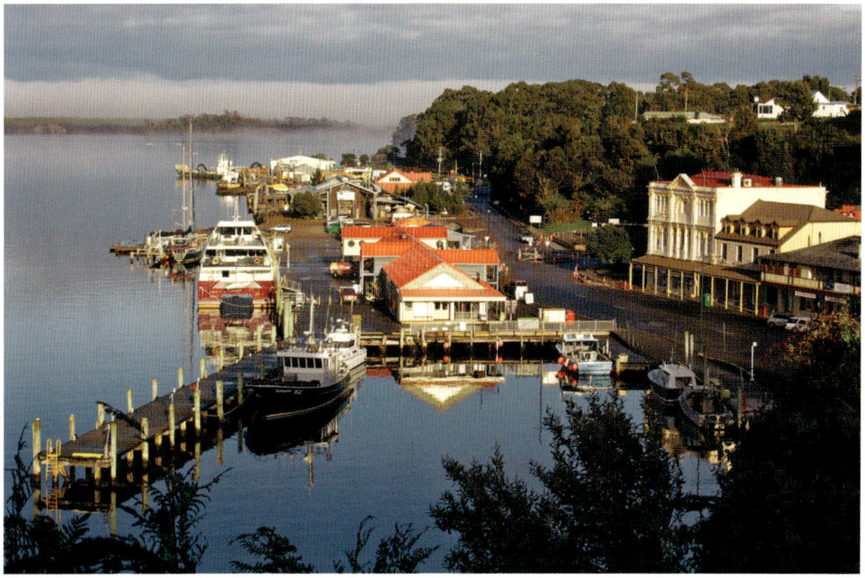

SOUTH WEST

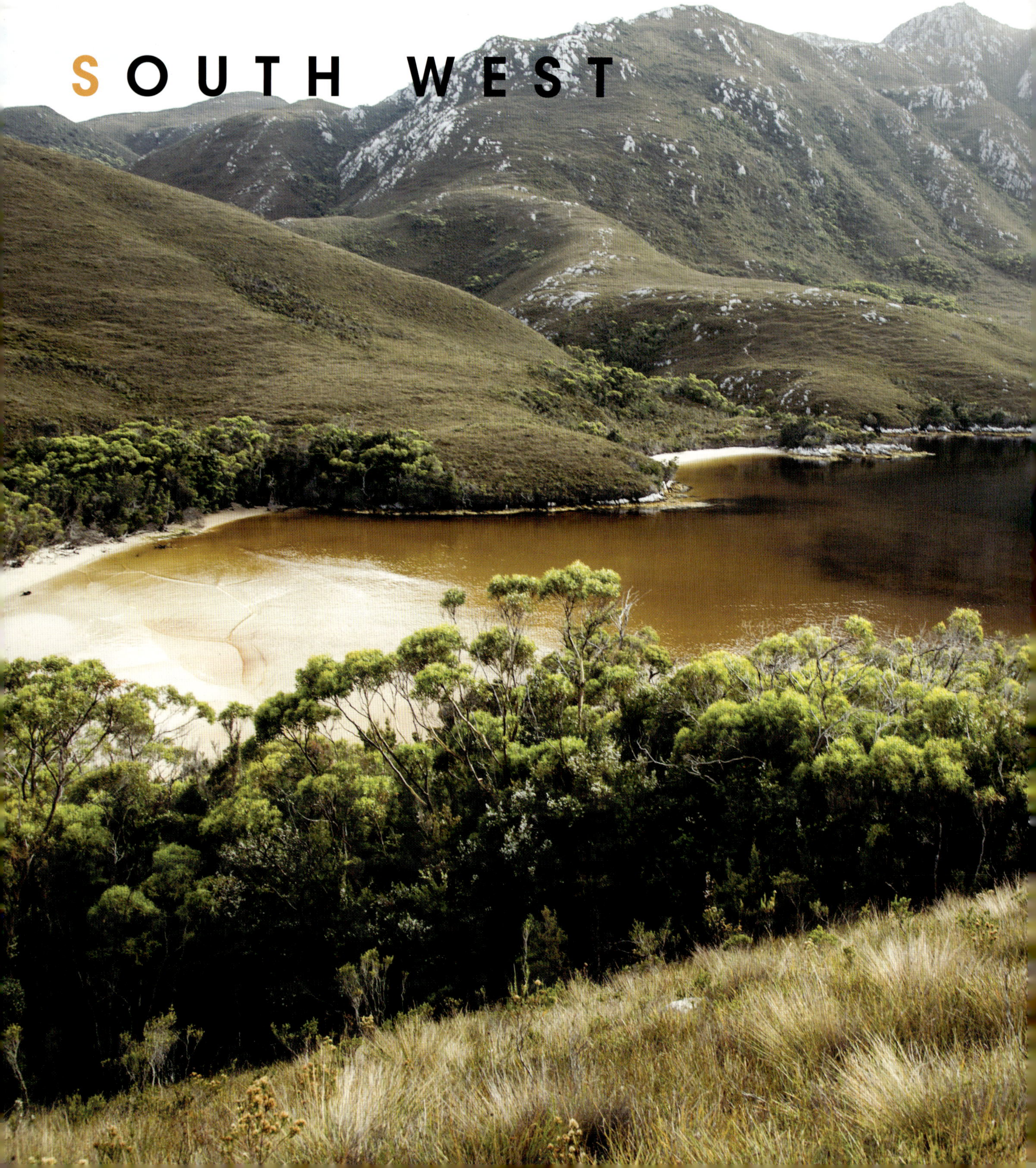

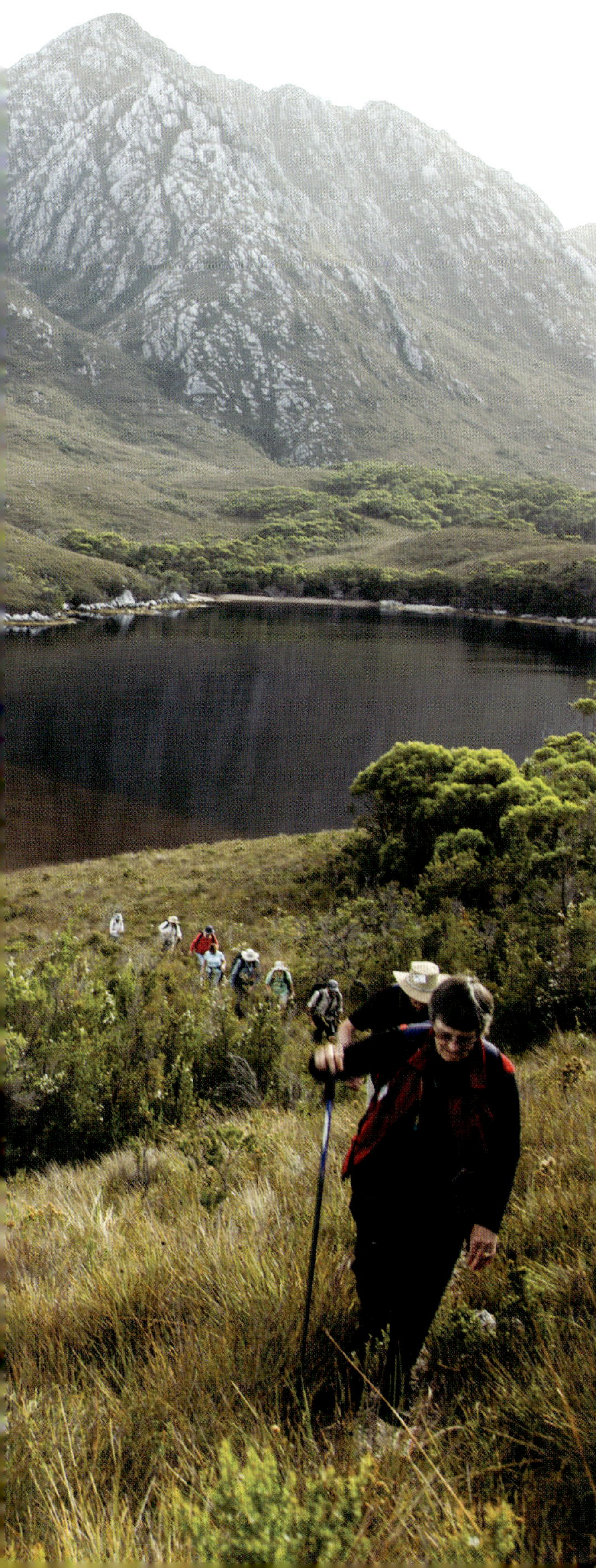

South West National Park is one of the wildest places on earth. The largest of Tasmania's national parks and part of the Wilderness World Heritage Area, it's a magnificent landscape of craggy mountain ranges, glacial lakes, alpine moorlands, buttongrass plains, ancient rainforest and a rugged southern coastline shaped by seas and winds roaring in from Antarctica. Naturally much of the park is incredibly remote and hard to see – here you will find the state's most challenging walks – but there are also a couple of places that can be accessed by car or plane. The northern part is traversed by the Gordon River Rd to Strathgordon but drop south onto the Scotts Peak Dam Road to get into the wilderness. The views from the Red Knoll lookout are astounding, taking in much of Lake Pedder and the Western Arthur Range. For walkers this is the start of the Western Arthur Traverse (70 km, 7 days), a beautiful but punishing circuit over the ranges that only the most experienced of bushwalkers attempt (see cover), and the Port Davey Track heading south to Port Davey and Melaleuca (70 km, 7 days). In the south, you can drive to Cockle Creek on Recherche Bay, the exit point of the South Coast Track. You can fly into Melaleuca to start the track or stay for a few days at Port Davey at the Southwest Wilderness Camp.

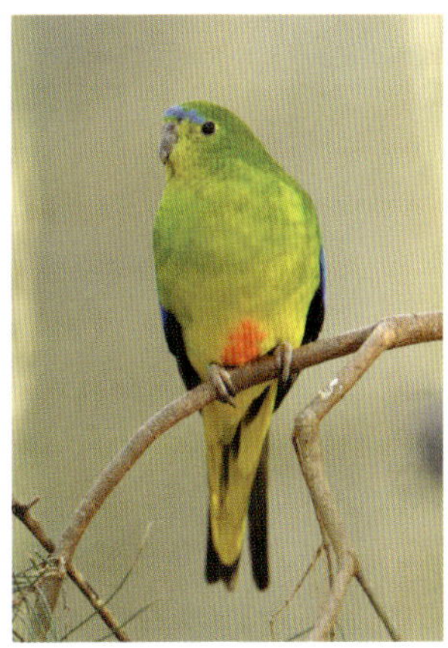

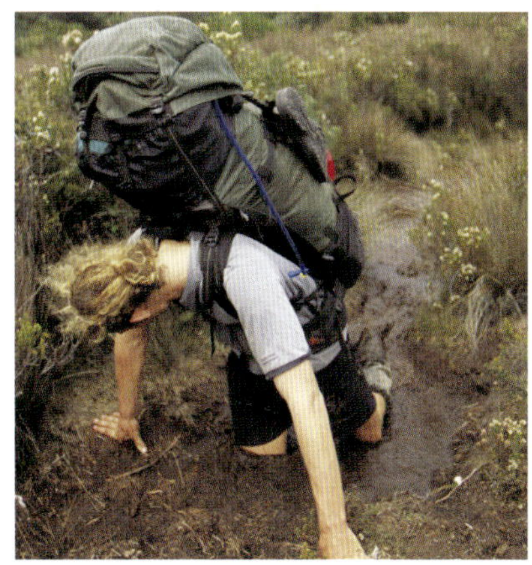

Left: The track to the top of Mt Milner (186 m) rises sharply from the tea-coloured waters of Bramble Cove, Port Davey.

Above left: On the brink of extinction, the Orange bellied parrot can be seen from a bird hide at Melaleuca.

Above right: The South Coast Track is a famously boggy 84-km 8-day walk from Melaleuca to Cockle Creek. You fly into Melaleuca but there are no huts or facilities so walkers must be completely self-sufficient. Guided tours are available for this walk and the Port Davey Track.

ACKNOWLEDGEMENTS

The author would like to thank all the talented photographers whose work is included here. She would particularly like to thank Chris Munn, Luke Tscharke and Arwen Dyer. Katrina would also like to thank Andrew Swaffer for his enthusiasm and commissioning the series; Christine Schiedel for her skill and patience; Jenny Cowan for the map, and Jo Runciman, Lauren Smith, Jess Teideman and Rebecca Cotton at Australian Geographic for their help. Thanks to Tourism Tasmania for their images. And finally, love and thanks always to Charlie Burrows.

ABOUT THE AUTHOR

Katrina O'Brien is the author of Australia's bestselling walking guide, *Sydney's Best Harbour & Coastal Walks*. She first fell in love with Tasmania, the Red Centre and the Kimberley while travelling and writing her way around Australia for two years as the co-author of the travel guides *Footprint Australia Handbook* and *Footprint West Coast Handbook*. When not researching and writing walking and travel guides Katrina is a book publishing consultant and has previously worked as Managing Editor for Murdoch Books and Penguin Lantern.

ABOUT THE PUBLISHERS

The Australian Geographic journal is a geographical magazine founded by Dick Smith in 1986. It mainly covers stories about Australia - its geography, culture, wildlife and people - and six editions are published every year. Australian Geographic also publish a number of books every year on similar subjects for both children and adults. A portion of the profits goes to the Australian Geographic Society which supports scientific research as well as environmental conservation, community projects and Australian adventurers.

Woodslane Press are a book publishing company based in Sydney, Australia. They are the publishers of Australia's best-selling walking guides and under their co-owned Boiling Billy imprint also publish camping, bush exploration and 4WD guides. For more than a decade committed to publishing books that empower Australians to better explore and understand their own country, Woodslane Press is proud to be working with Australian Geographic to produce this new series of souvenir books.

Also available:

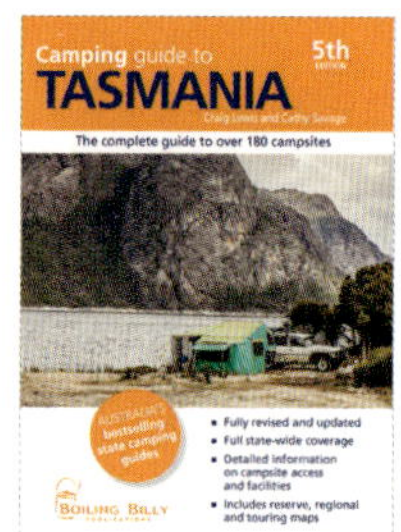

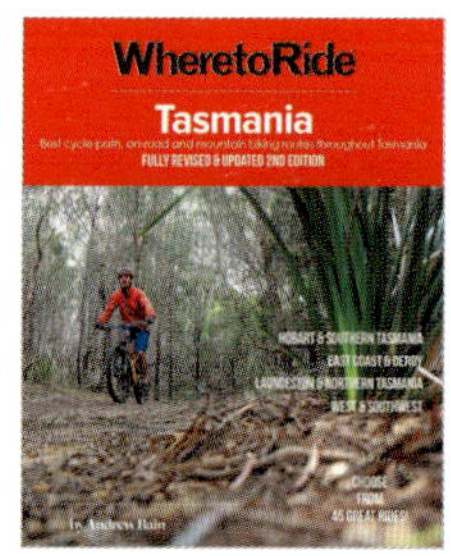

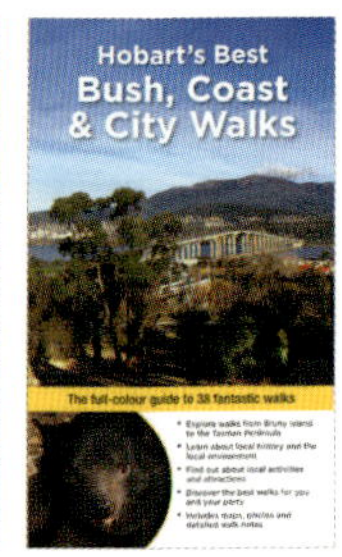

PICTURE CREDITS

pi: James_Stone76/ Shutterstock (Aurora Australis over Betsey Island just south of Hobart)
pii: Australian Geographic (Crossing New River lagoon outlet, South Coast Track)
p1: Justin Gilligan/Australian Geographic (Hermit crab on bull kelp just off Maria Island)
p2-3 sandergroffen/iStock
p5: D. Parer & E. Parer-Cook/Minden Pictures/Alamy Stock Photo
p6-7: Luke Tscharke/Australian Geographic (main); Australian Geographic (fossils)
p9: keiichihiki/iStock
p10: tsvibrav/iStock
p11: Bill Bachman/Australian Geographic (top); Ian Connellan/Australian Geographic (bottom)
p12: JurgaR/iStock
p13: Justin Gilligan/Australian Geographic
p14-15: Luke Tscharke/Australian Geographic
p16: Cameron Cope/Australian Geographic
p17: D. Parer & E. Parer-Cook/Minden Pictures/Alamy Stock Photo (rosella); keiichihiki/ iStock (echidna); Mitch Reardon/ Australian Geographic (quoll)
p18-19: Rob Burnett/Tourism Tasmania (kangaroos); Justin Gilligan/Australian Geographic (fish); Tim Dub/Australian Geographic (penguins); Ian Connellan/ Australian Geographic (devil)
p20: Bill Hatcher/National Geographic Image Collection / Alamy Stock Photo
p21: Shane Pedersen/Alamy Stock Photo (top); Katrina O'Brien (bottom left & bottom right); Don Fuchs/Australian Geographic (bottom middle)
p22-23: Boyloso/iStock
p24: Alastair Bett/Tourism Tasmania
p25: Adam Gibson/Tourism Tasmania (top); Redzaal/iStock (bottom)
p26-27: Matthew Newton/Australian Geographic
p28: Katrina O'Brien
p29: Andrew Swaffer (top); Ian Connellan/ Australian Geographic (bottom)
p30-31: Martin Willis/Minden Pictures/Alamy Stock Photo (bird); Tim Dub/Australian Geographic (beach); Rob Burnett/Tourism Tasmania (Commissariat)
p32-33: Luke Tscharke
p34-35: Oliver_Koch/ iStock (main); mishrobinson/iStock (right)
p36: Courtesy of Tasmanian Walking Company
p37: Esther Beaton/Australian Geographic (wombat); Benny Marty/Shutterstock (rocks)
p38-39: Chris Munn (main); Shmenny50/ iStock (detail)
p40-41: Peripitus/Commons Wikimedia (main); Ian Connellan/Australian Geographic (devil)
p42-43: Ian Woolcock/Alamy Stock Photo
p44-45: Luke Wait Photography/iStock (main); Katrina O'Brien (detail)
p46-47: keiichihiki/ iStock (main); /Rob Burnett/ Tourism Tasmania (pademelons)
p48-49: Simonology/iStock
p50: David Bristow/Australian Geographic
p51: Bildagentur Zoonar GmbH/Shutterstock (top); David Bristow/Australian Geographic (bottom)
p52-53: Arwen Dyer (main); Michael R Evans/ Shutterstock (Stanley)
p54-55: Pete Harmsen/Tourism Tasmania (main); Dan Broun (crayfish)
p56-57: Graham Freeman/Tourism Australia/ World Heritage Cruises
p58-59: Chris Munn (main); Owen Derrick/Alamy Stock Photo (Strahan)
p60-61: Chrissie Goldrick/Australian Geographic (main); quentinjlang/iStock (bird); Australian Geographic (walker)